Also by Shelley Fraser Mickle

Babaro: America's Horse

AMERICAN PHAROAH

TRIPLE CROWN CHAMPION

Shelley Fraser Mickle

ALADDIN

New York   London   Toronto   Sydney   New Delhi

❤ ALADDIN

An imprint of Simon & Schuster Children's Publishing Division

1230 Avenue of the Americas, New York, New York 10020

First Aladdin hardcover edition March 2017

For information about special discounts for bulk purchases, please contact

Simon & Schuster Special Sales at 1-866-506-1949 or business@simonandschuster.com.

The Simon & Schuster Speakers Bureau can bring authors to your live event.

For more information or to book an event contact the Simon & Schuster Speakers Bureau

at 1-866-248-3049 or visit our website at www.simonspeakers.com.

Jacket designed by Karin Paprocki, Karina Granda, and Nina Simoneaux

Interior designed by Nina Simoneaux

The text of this book was set in Bembo Std.

Manufactured in the United States of America 0217 FFG

10 9 8 7 6 5 4 3 2 1

Library of Congress Control Number 2016944564

ISBN 978-1-4814-8070-3 (hc)

ISBN 978-1-4814-8072-7 (eBook)

CONTENTS

JUNE 6, 2015

THEY SAID HE couldn't do it. They said he wouldn't win.

They seemed to be everywhere: pessimists and naysayers in newspapers, in sports magazines and on the Internet. Sure, he was an impressive three-year-old horse, this American Pharoah who first became famous for having a misspelled name and a chewed-off tail. But no way would he be a Triple Crown winner, winning three races in five weeks—the Kentucky Derby, the Preakness, the Belmont Stakes. The reasons were longer than a chore list.

- So what if he *does* have the great Secretariat in his bloodline? His mother was a sprinter. He doesn't have what it takes to go a mile and a half in the Belmont.
- Look at his times! His final quarter mile in his Kentucky Derby win was a crawling 26.57 seconds. That's like a kiddie car on a freeway.
- Other greats—Seattle Slew, Citation, Count Fleet— those Triple Crown winners were old-timey Thorough-breds, bred to be heartier, stronger, tougher. This kid, Pharoah, will be toast.

- Today, no horse can handle that schedule—win the Kentucky Derby, then two weeks later, the Preakness, and after only a three-week rest, win the longest race of them all, the Belmont, with its grueling one and a half miles. The first two take too much out of them; they need recovery time.
- If a truly great horse, Spectacular Bid, couldn't get it done in 1979, don't expect any horse to secure American horse racing's most coveted sweep. After all, in his career, Spectacular Bid ran thirty races and won twenty-six, and one of his only losses was the Belmont. The Triple Crown is the hardest prize to win in all American sports. It hasn't been done in thirty-seven years. Sorry, Pharoah, nice try, but you're running against history.
- If he doesn't draw a good post position for tactical advantage, it's, *So long, Pharoah, it was nice to know ya.*
- The best recipe for a Triple Crown is a truly great horse in a weak year. American Pharoah might be a great horse, but this is not a weak year.

Even a scientific study before the Belmont showed why American Pharoah would not win. It cited glycogen levels used up during intense exercise. It pointed out that the muscle power used in his wins in the Kentucky Derby and Preakness would not have had time to repair. And then there was the point about the wear and tear on a Thoroughbred's skeleton.

Poor Pharoah. He was called a loser before he even began.

Only eleven horses had won the Triple Crown. Yet in the midst of this time when *It can't be done* was a cool thing to say, a dark brown horse walked into the starting gate to change America's mind.

Some would never want to admit that they needed this: to behold a breathing half-wild creature with a heart born of willingness to burst through history. In this time when meanness, bullying, shooting down dreams, and worrying about the world rose from frustration and confusion to look smart in agreeing to nothing, something was about to happen. It was the sort of thing that appears only once in a great while—as when Mozart sat down at a piano or Michelangelo put his brush to the ceiling at the Sistine Chapel and his sculpting tool to a hunk of stone. A miracle was about to happen.

That is, for those who took the time to look.

Victor Espinoza, five foot two, worn from his forty-three years of outrunning poverty, hunkered in the saddle on the back of American Pharoah in the starting gate and heard his stomach growl. Today he had already ridden a handful of races, and now he was about to take off in the big one. *The Big one, the Belmont for the Triple Crown.* "Don't think of it;

you might jinx yourself," he silently coached himself. But boy, was he hungry!

Usually he had two rituals on race day: to take a nap and to pray. He prayed for safety and health. He napped to conserve energy. But today he'd had no time for a nap. Yet how much good would a nap really do? Excitement about the chance to win the Triple Crown would have peppered his *z*'s. Besides, he'd been here twice before. And each time, winning had eluded him.

When he talked to himself, he often used Spanish, the language he had grown up with. Born in the town of Tulancingo in the state of Hidalgo, Mexico, on May 23, 1972, one of twelve children, he was now surprised to be the oldest jockey in this race. For someone who grew up taking care of goats—leading them up a mountain before school so they could eat all day, then going all the way up again to bring them back before supper—he'd learned long ago never to have dreams. Dreams could break your heart. But goals—now, having goals was a different matter. And here he was, fulfilling one of his highest: riding in the Belmont, going for the Triple Crown for the third time. Most never even got a first chance.

The others that he'd ridden in the Belmont Stakes with

a chance at the Triple Crown were splendid horses, the best of the best: War Emblem in 2002 and California Chrome in 2014. But California Chrome had come up short in the stretch. War Emblem had stumbled coming out of the starting gate, totally jinxing his chances, ending up eighth. Oh, that moment at the start! It could mean everything, and Pharoah himself liked to shift his feet in the starting gate. *What if . . . No. One mustn't go there—not to the badlands of "what could happen."*

Besides, this time felt a bit different. In the year that he and American Pharoah had been a team, he had not yet asked the big bay colt for his highest gear, his greatest speed. No one really knew what the colt was capable of. Even more unusual than his blazing speed was the colt's temperament. Often young racehorse stallions are so aggressive that being around them requires handlers to watch out for their fingers and toes. Aggressive young horses can bite as quickly as a rattlesnake strike. They can whirl about at the drop of a leaf to land on someone's toes. While Pharoah could be aggressive around other horses and as nervous as a feral barn cat—especially since he was sensitive to the noise of a crowd—Victor had found that Pharoah was also so gentle and trusting that the young horse could actually fall asleep in his arms. And here Victor was about to ask this kind creature to put away a field of seven aggressive three-year-old Thoroughbreds and stomp open the pages of racehorse history.

In the starting gate, post position five, American Pharoah shifted his feet as usual—right, left, and then back. The big bay horse didn't know that a trophy waited at the end of the track. He didn't know what money was. He didn't know about a human's hunt for glory. Even if he had known, he wouldn't have cared. He simply had to trust and obey the human on his back, who was only necessary as the supporting player to release what was never quenched: the urge to run, to run. It didn't even matter where.

The challenge now was to wait. Three more horses had to load for this total field of eight. A big Thoroughbred named Frammento was in the starting gate on his left. Now on his right, the impressive gray, Frosted, was led in, followed by the click of the gate tucking him in.

Thank goodness for the earplugs to snuff out most of the noise; otherwise Pharoah was likely to go bonkers now. After his first race, it had been discovered that he was supersensitive to sound, which could set off an anxiety that would use him up. So always now, he wore earplugs.

The seats were all sold out. The crowd had been limited to ninety thousand. Most of those were now on tiptoe, their sense of excitement passing from one to the other in a heightening roar. Not many in the crowd—along with some twenty million others watching on television—*really* expected to see a winner break the long Triple Crown dry spell. Three decades of seeing twelve horses qualify for the Crown by winning both the Kentucky Derby and Preakness but fail to win the Belmont had tempered racehorse fans' expectations. In 2012 a horse ironically named I'll Have Another could have made the elite list of contenders thirteen, but he had been scratched from the Belmont with an injury.

Yet, despite the dry spell of having no Triple Crown winner since 1978 with Affirmed, and the year before with Seattle Slew, those who *were* there quietly held on to the possibility of seeing something breathtakingly spectacular. In the back of everyone's mind was the fervent hope to see a win like that of Secretariat in 1973. That was the year the big chestnut put away a field of contenders by a freakish thirty-one lengths. While claiming the Triple Crown trophy and a blanket of carnations in stunning glory, Secretariat also set a track record.

Yes, it was always fun to be at the Belmont Stakes for the excitement of the famous race. And, of course, for the party.

Victor was thinking about the one-eighth pole. He knew that when he and Pharoah got there, he could sense how much Pharoah had left—how much strength, how much desire, how much fight to take over the lead of this small herd as if he were living out his fantasy of running wild on a far-off prairie. That desire thrived deep in the colt's instinctual memory. What would set it loose could be a matter of Victor's riding, positioning the colt to receive a silent signal sent between rivals. It could be the threat from one young stallion to another, sending the message, *Don't you dare pass,* which was the standard challenge of one alpha horse to another.

If Victor could coach Pharoah into that long, smooth-as-silk cruising speed and keep a lookout for who was coming up behind, he could take note of how Pharoah was breathing. In his jockey's stance, his ankles would be in contact with the colt's big chest, and through his boots he would feel Pharoah's heartbeat. That would tell him the colt's stamina. Then Pharoah could send back his signals of, *I got this, Coach. No sweat. This herd is mine!*

Through the six races they had already won together, the language they had built between them became like two musicians blending the notes of their separate training. Pharoah's trainers had taught him to *rate*, to use his speed in response to the shift of the jockey's body and the grip on the reins. Rating his speed saved his stamina for the home-stretch and was also essential to carrying out a race strategy. Maneuvering among the field for the final turn to the finish line could be tricky. It always required that a horse listen and obey its jockey.

Through their first few races, Victor had learned to read Pharoah's silent language—an instant message sent through a twitch of the young horse's ears, through a tenseness of muscle. Hundreds of small unconscious readings were now being taken in by both man and horse. They were two athletes on countdown, primed for blastoff.

The last post position was filled, and the gate clicked behind Materiality, the horse many believed would steal the race. They'd met up once before—Pharoah and this son of Afleet Alex, the horse who in 2005 had stumbled to his knees in the stretch of the Preakness and won anyway. Then he'd even gone on to win the Belmont. A tough, tough horse! What if his son had inherited that burning desire to overcome anything, and used that grit today? Clearly, there was stellar competition for Pharoah.

Victor concentrated; Pharoah read Victor's body tensing, and like a good dance partner, the colt coiled himself in response, leaning a little against the back gate. *Oh no!* The trainer had told Victor to put Pharoah on the lead, to get out front at the start and stay there.

Mess up the break from the gate, and they would both be a dot in history.

The starting bell sounded with a harsh burr, and the gates swung open. As American Pharoah leaped out, he was a step behind the others due to leaning against the back gate, and his pace was a little slow. Victor urged him to understand that getting out front now was the most important thing in the world.

As if frozen in flight, Pharoah stretched out, his hooves seeming to barely skim the track. Suspended in air, he began his next stride.

At the one-eighth pole, Victor took note: yes, Pharoah was breathing like a happy, well-stocked steam engine. Underneath his left boot, he felt Pharoah's heartbeat. It was pumping in a fine rhythm—a strong, robust two-beat thump. The trick now was to conserve that strength, to know where everyone else on the track was, and not to ask Pharoah for more speed until, until . . .

Around them, hoof-thunder rose in a roar: a sound as awe-inspiring as any on earth. Even the ground itself seemed to tremble in the onrush of so much power. In the midst of it all, Victor was smiling. American Pharoah certainly seemed ready to shake history in his teeth, pry it open, and sail through.

◢ WHY WINNING A TRIPLE CROWN IS SO RARE ◣

To win a Triple Crown, a young three-year-old Thoroughbred must win three races in a grueling schedule of only five weeks. The first race is the Kentucky Derby, on the first Saturday in May in Louisville, Kentucky. It is limited to a field of twenty horses to run for a mile and a quarter, and all those twenty have to earn points to enter, which means that only the best three-year-olds of that year are running.

Two weeks later is the Preakness Stakes in Baltimore, Maryland, for a distance of a mile and three-sixteenths. Even though that distance is shorter than the Derby— and the field is usually small—those running are again the best of the three-year-olds, fit and ready to race. If a horse is victorious in both of those legs of the Triple Crown, then three weeks later that horse faces the longest race of all, the Belmont Stakes, a mile and a half. The order of these races has been the same since 1931.

No wonder the Belmont, this last jewel in the

Triple Crown races, has been nicknamed "The Test of the Champion." Inaugurated in 1867, the first Belmont Stakes was held in the Bronx, one of the five boroughs of New York City. It was named after horse-racing enthusiast August Belmont Sr., who financed the first race. In 1905 it was moved to a new 430-acre racetrack in Elmont, New York, on Long Island just outside New York City.

The race is held on the first Saturday that falls on or after June 5. The winning horse is draped with a blanket of white carnations after the race, similar to the tradition of the Kentucky Derby winner being draped in roses and the Preakness winner being draped in black-eyed Susans.

In the winner's circle, the owner of the winning horse is given a silver trophy designed by the famous Tiffany & Co. in New York City. This trophy was first presented to August Belmont Sr. in 1869 and was donated by the Belmont family for each year's presentation since 1926.

At its mile-and-a-half-length on a dirt track, the Belmont is open to only three-year-old Thoroughbreds, either colts, geldings, or fillies—though it is rare for a filly to be entered in a race against male horses. The word *colt* describes a male horse under the age of three. When a colt turns three, he is then considered to be a *stallion*, though racehorse people tend to say "three-year-old colt." A *gelding* is a male horse that has been fixed so as not to breed. *Fillies* are female horses until they are three, when they are called *mares*. In general, colts and geldings are stronger and more mature than fillies at the beginning of their race careers. Colts and geldings in the Triple Crown races carry 126 pounds; fillies carry 121 pounds.

SHELLEY FRASER MICKLE

The term *graded stakes race* means any Thorough-bred horse race in the United States or Canada that requires an entry fee that owners must pay. The term has been used since 1973 by the Thoroughbred Owners and Breeders Association, which also grades the stakes into three levels, I, II, and III, always using roman numerals to identify them. The fees to enter, added to an additional amount from the racetrack, make up the prize money paid to first-, second-, third-, and fourth-place finishers. All of the Triple Crown races are Grade I stakes.

In 1930 a horse-racing columnist for the *New York Times*, Bryan Field, noted that in America the three races—the Kentucky Derby, the Preakness, and the Belmont Stakes—had reached such prominence that all other races for three-year-old Thoroughbreds were overshadowed. He wrote, "To win the Triple Crown in America carries with it the utmost that can be won on our racecourses."

By 1935, when the Thoroughbred Omaha won the three races, more writers picked up the term in describing that horse's accomplishment. Two years later when War Admiral won all three races, the term *Triple Crown* was everywhere.

On the rare occasion that a horse has won all three races, the Triple Crown trophy—a silver vase first awarded to winner Citation in 1948—is presented in the winner's circle at the Belmont. Winning the Triple Crown is indeed an extraordinary feat for a young Thoroughbred.

2

GROUNDHOG DAY WITH LITTLEPRINCESSEMMA

ON FEBRUARY 2, 2012, Groundhog Day at Stockplace Farm outside Lexington, Kentucky, veterinarian Tom VanMeter got a call from the foaling barn at eleven that night. The mare named Littleprincessemma was in labor. She was named after her owner's daughter, Emma, with the letters all smashed together to fit into the eighteen spaces required to register a Thoroughbred.

Dr. VanMeter expected such calls at that time of year. His farm of eight hundred acres was the birthplace of some forty foals each late winter or early spring. Most were born at night, since nature intended that by daylight the newborns would be on their feet, ready to run from danger, if necessary.

Now the almost six-year-old chestnut mare Littleprincessemma lay in the deep straw of her stall. At precisely eleven fifteen, she pushed out an unremarkable brown colt.

Following the instincts she was born with, Little-princessemma reached back to sniff and nudge her newborn baby to see if he was alive. She had given birth to one other foal, so she was a little more accustomed to how all this went. Her chestnut coat was sticky and wet from the birth. Now both mother and baby were ready to follow the script written deep in their instinctual behaviors over the thousands of years that horses had been on earth.

Those watching—the farm manager, the vet, a barn worker—stepped respectfully back, becoming still and quiet for these first critical moments of bonding between mother and baby.

At this time of year in Kentucky, foals are born just before the bluish blades of grass pop up in spring. The limestone beneath the ground enriches the grass and water. Natural minerals make young Thoroughbred horses strong, strengthening their bones and plumping their bodies into half-ton wonders that seem to grow wings on their feet from an inborn love of speed.

The birth of any baby is a wondrous event when nature lifts its veil to reveal its secrets by directing the show. In the first hour of his life, this bay colt was a willing captive of his instincts. After a little shuffling in the straw, he quickly propped himself up on his chest. Then he let out a high tinkling whinny—the sort of sound that makes humans chuckle. And smiles linger.

The colt shook his head and snorted. While the gesture seemed endearing, it was actually a reflex to clear his nose. Immediately, the hairlike fingers of cilia beat inside his lungs and up his airways to sweep the passages clear. He could breathe easily now.

Shimmying around to the side of his mother, he moved enough to break the cord between them. That attachment to his mother's placenta had kept him alive for the eleven months that he had grown inside her. That umbilical lifeline had brought him the nutrients he needed, and now the broken cord dangled from each of them.

Everyone waited to see the critical moment. The colt needed to stand up. The mare was already up. If some danger threatened, she had to get him ready to run. Even in a stall, surrounded by people who would never knowingly let anything bad happen to them, the mare could not dismiss her instincts. On the chance that a predator—a bobcat, wolves, or a mountain lion—took chase, following their own instincts to bite their prey's ankles, aiming for a grip to pull a horse down and especially a foal—she had to be prepared. Littleprincessemma's plans for her newborn foal did not include his being a mountain lion's lunch.

So, stand up, stand up quickly, she signaled over and over by nudging him.

Suddenly the colt shivered—a good sign. Shivering showed that in his brain, which acted as his thermostat, he was being sent the signal to use his muscles to warm up.

He then stuck out his tongue. He made a sucking noise. With that cue, Littleprincessemma began biting her foal. It was her way again to urge him to stand up.

Now the brown colt was struggling to his feet. But as soon as he was up, he fell. Then he fell again. Falling was good; it was also a part of nature's script, for the force of it slapped fluid from his lungs. Now up and nudging his mother, he was driven to look for what he knew he had to have to survive.

He sucked the air. He sucked his mother's hip. He sucked her shoulder. When she nudged him, pushing him toward her udder, where the warm milk already dripped, he grabbed it with a ravenous hunger. The milk streamed into his mouth and dribbled onto his chin.

Now Dr. VanMeter stepped forward to check out both

mother and baby. As incongruous as it seems, horses are as fragile as they are strong. Vegetarians and as powerful as a tractor, they have strange plumbing. Their intestines form a one-way system that is not built for regurgitation—which is a fancy way of saying they can't throw up. What goes down must keep moving, and heaven forbid that it should be a poisonous weed or a wad of sand to clog up the works.

With the use of a stethoscope, Dr. VanMeter listened for gut sounds in Littleprincessemma. He checked her heart and made sure the placenta had been passed. Then he checked over the foal and toweled him off. All signs said he was healthy too.

Since the colt's wiry coat was drying, it could be seen that there were no markings of white anywhere—not on his feet, not on his face. A star seemed to have formed on his forehead, but then changed its mind and sped off, leaving a white swirl like a faint footprint.

He had no name. He had no distinguishing markings. He was one of the 21,725 Thoroughbred foals to be registered in the United States that year. His future was as much a mystery as the secrets that had brought him here.

But then, we all know, another truth would shape this

story. The promise of greatness was there. It always is.

A barn worker turned off the lights. A door closed. Everyone went back to bed or to their nighttime jobs. The mare and her newborn stood in their stall, serene, bonded, and busy with living.

American Pharoah's father's name, Pioneerof the Nile, was registered with the letters running together to fit the Jockey Club's requirements of eighteen characters

AMERICAN PHAROAH'S PEDIGREE		
AMERICAN PHAROAH	PIONEEROF THE NILE (USA) 2006, dkb/br.	EMPIRE MAKER (USA) 2000, dkb/br.
		STAR OF GOSHEN (USA) 1994, b.
	LITTLEPRINCESSEMMA (USA) 2006, ch.	YANKEE GENTLEMAN (USA) 1999, b.
		EXCLUSIVE ROSETTE (USA) 1993, ch.

only, including spaces. In the grid below, the year following the horse's name means the year of its birth. *Dkb/br.* stands for dark bay or brown; *ch.* stands for chestnut.

UNBRIDLED (USA) 1987, b.	FAPPIANO (USA) 1977, b.	MR. PROSPECTOR (USA) 1970
		KILLALOE (USA) 1970
	GANA FACIL (USA) 1981, ch.	LE FABULEUX (FR) 1961
		CHAREDI (USA) 1976
TOUSSAUD (USA) 1989, b.	EL GRAN SENOR (USA) 1981, b.	NORTHERN DANCER (CAN) 1961
		SEX APPEAL (USA) 1970
	IMAGE OF REALITY (USA) 1976, b.	IN REALITY (USA) 1964
		EDEE's IMAGE (USA) 1969
LORD AT WAR (USA) 1980, ch.	GENERAL (FR) 1974, b.	BRIGADIER GERARD (GD) 1968
		MERCUIALE (FR) 1965
	LUNA DE MIEL (ARG) 1974, ch.	CON BRIO (GB) 1961
		GOOD WILL (ARG) 1965
CASTLE EIGHT (USA) 1987, dkb/br.	KEY TO THE KINGDOM (USA) 1970, dkb/br.	BOLD RULER (USA) 1954
		KEY BRIDGE (USA) 1959
	HER NATIVE (USA) 1973, b.	KANUMERA (USA) 1966
		LITTLE BLESSING (USA) 1964
STORM CAT (USA) 1983, br.	STORM BIRD (CAN) 1978, b.	NORTHERN DANCER (CAN) 1961
		SOUTH OCEAN (CAN) 1967
	TERLINGUA (USA) 1976, ch.	SECRETARIAT (USA) 1970
		CRIMSON SAINT (USA) 1969
KEY PHRASE (USA) 1991, ch.	FLYING PASTER (USA) 1976, b.	GUMMO (USA) 1962
		PROCNE (USA) 1969
	SOWN (USA) 1983, ch.	GRENFALL (USA) 1968
		BAD SEED (USA) 1969
ECLIPTICAL (USA) 1982, ch.	EXCLUSIVE NATIVE (USA) 1965, ch.	RAISE A NATIVE (USA) 1961
		EXCLUSIVE (USA) 1953
	MINNETONKA (USA) 1967, b.	CHIEFTAIN (USA) 1961
		HELIOLIGHT (USA) 1957
ZETTA JET (USA) 1984, b.	TRI JET (USA) 1969, blk/br.	JESTER (USA) 1955
		HAZE (USA) 1953
	QUEEN ZETTA (USA) 1976, ch.	CROZIER (USA) 1958
		MIAMI MOOD (USA) 1961

3

BEWARE OF THE BILLIES

THIRTY-FIVE YEARS BEFORE, in Hidalgo, Mexico, on a goat farm, five-year-old Victor dragged himself out of bed at sunrise and rushed to help his brothers. There were five of them, five brothers. Of the twelve Espinoza children, Victor was next to the youngest. Between the boys, it was their job to get the goats up the mountain behind the farm to graze all day.

There were a lot of them. Hundreds of goats—hundreds!

Shooing them, pushing them forward, heading off strays—it was no small job. It had to be done quickly, too, because the boys had to get to school.

Herding them out of the corral behind the house, Victor and his brothers used sticks and their hands and their high-pitched boys' voices—calling out in Spanish, "Shoo, go, go on, get!"

Once the goats were up the mountain, the brothers rushed home to have breakfast. Then it was off to school.

Before sunset, it was their job to get all the goats back down again. As they herded them into the corral behind the house, they counted them. Not one could be lost.

Each one meant money for the family. The nannies meant milk and cheese. But the billy goats, oh, those billies—more than once Victor was butted to the ground. He scrambled up, brushing off dust as he ran to keep from being butted again. He learned to call back some pretty harsh things to those billies, too.

Then, after supper, if there was any daylight left before bed, the brothers would play racquetball against a patio wall. Since they had no racquets, they used their hands.

There was one unexpected benefit to caring for all those goats—one that Victor never would have thought of. For when he went to kindergarten, he found that he was a whiz at math. Doing long addition was nothing compared to counting goats. Thinking in numbers was as natural to him as breathing.

Always, he and his five brothers could think up some wild things to do. Climbing up on cows, donkeys, goats, and sheep, they'd bet on who could stay on the longest. Without a watch to measure the seconds, they counted: *one Mississippi, two Mississippi* . . . but of course they were counting in Spanish. And then *wham!* they'd go sailing off when the cow, donkey, goat, or sheep got fed up and bucked, pitching the brothers, one at a time, onto to the ground like bags of dirty laundry.

It was a miracle that Victor never broke a bone.

Life was hard. Rewards were few. But the constant chatter of twelve children, and all the things they could think up to do, meant that Victor was never alone. There were happy times of bunching together to sleep at night, of shoving to find a place at the dinner table, and of playing makeshift games, in which getting blissfully dirty was part of the fun.

Victor had always been small. And while he was naturally playful with a sunny disposition, he quickly learned that being compliant and funny were good defenses too. As the next to youngest in a line of older brothers, he was sometimes picked on and teased.

Before he was eight, he began to know—and to know so as never to forget—that he would not get through life without being tough. He developed a stubborn inner core to shield himself from unkind attacks and the natural slaps of living. He was learning how to take care of himself.

His days were their own timepiece: up with the goats,

down with the goats. Church, school, ride a goat or donkey—at least for a count of five. Few other events interrupted the cycle.

Then, when he turned eight, a sudden death unhinged his world. Sitting in church with his eleven brothers and sisters near his father's coffin, he did not know how to think about this loss. It was as if the planet had stopped in its orbit and shuddered for a moment, so now the whole family struggled to keep their balance.

Behind a veil, his mother's face was frozen in sorrow. He did not know how to comfort her.

Over time, he began to know—to sense in a way that he could not have explained: survival would become the mountain he climbed each day. Poverty was one step closer to chasing him down.

Stay or run. Leave or stay. But to where? How?

The choice was not pretty. The thought of it was agony.

4

SPEED LAPS AND HOOF SPINS

THE UNNAMED COLT, turned out in a pasture on Stockplace Farm in Lexington, Kentucky, with his mother, Littleprincessemma, leaped in the crisp air. He tore around the pasture with his gang of other foals, and then flopped down next to his mother in the stubby grass to bask in the lemony sun.

The Groundhog Day on which the colt had been born had not been one to break the winter. In Punxsutawney, Pennsylvania, where the Groundhog Day ritual is practiced, at 7:25 a.m. that year, the chosen groundhog was rooted out of his burrow to look for his shadow. Supposedly he saw it and scampered back into his hole. Seeing his shadow meant the groundhog predicted six more weeks of winter.

Now, three weeks later, in a pasture in Lexington, Kentucky, the little brown colt saw his shadow and was so spooked by it that he jumped in the air as if stuck with a hot poker. After a few minutes of whizzing around the pasture, he seemed to decide that the shadow of himself had been safely outrun. But instead of slowing down, he ran out of sheer horse-joy. With a buck here and there, he punctuated his pasture speed lap much like a good cook throws spices into a bubbling stew.

He liked the cold air. All he needed to know was that his mother was nearby.

As the weeks passed, he took longer and longer run-abouts from her. Turning to find her, he would spin on his back hooves and come leaping and bucking back, defying gravity in catlike leaps and reveling in what his gangly legs could do. As if testing them over and over, he would stiffen them, catapult himself off the ground, do a few aerial tricks for the fun of it, and then, much like a kitten, take every opportunity to pretend to be spooked again.

There was much he had been learning.

He knew to accept the halter put on his head with its straps of leather. He learned that a lead rope could be slipped through it—a special slip rope for safety—and that he should follow whoever was holding it. That is not always an easy thing to learn. Being led meant he swallowed his fear and trusted the human hooked to him.

When he was only a week old, his mother had been tested every day to see when she would come into *foal heat*, which was the short time when she could become pregnant again. On the day when she was found to be most likely to become pregnant, she was led into the barn with him following her. He was put in a stall opposite another foal and its dam while his own mother was led to a trailer to be driven forty minutes away to mate again with his father, Pioneerof the Nile.

While his mother was gone, looking across at the mare and foal opposite him provided comfort. Then, at the end of the day, his mother was brought back. She now had the chance of carrying nature's gift of a foal to be born that next spring.

Once again, life for the little brown colt was made up of days when the spin and leap of his legs was a never-ending discovery. It was a discovery that was sheer joy—empowering, fun, safe, and always secure beside his mother.

The promise that lay within him—in his bones, muscles, and heart—was not yet of a kind to be recognized as unique. He was simply celebrating being alive. He was also an athlete exploring his toolbox.

Foal is the term given to any young horse less than a year old. After its first birthday, the foal is then called a *yearling*. The mare after she gives birth is known as the foal's *dam*. Seven to twelve days after a dam has given birth is the time when she is most fertile. This short window when she can get pregnant again is called *foal heat*.

Those who breed horses are always eager to catch the *foal heat* of the mare's first estrus cycle after giving birth, when an egg is released to be fertilized in her womb.

Since horses are pregnant for eleven months, they need to have their babies in nonthreatening weather. So catching *foal heat* to breed to a stallion is not only desirable, but it can also mean life or death for a baby. *Foal heat* is nature's way to protect horses in the wild, since they then almost always have babies at the end of winter when the weather will soon become mild.

After a stallion fathers a baby, he is known as the *sire*. A stallion kept for breeding is known as a *stud*, and he is sometimes described as *standing at stud*.

With horse racing, there had to be some way to avoid the confusion of horses with different birthdays being eligible to race as they began their careers. So the Jockey Club, the principal governing body of horse racing, made the rule that all Thoroughbred babies would be registered with the same birthday of January 1, no matter in which month they were born. Then, after turning two, by February 1, they all must be named and registered with the Jockey Club.

As a way to control the number of Thoroughbreds born each year, rules restrict the way that mares become pregnant. The Thoroughbred breed is the only breed requiring mares to always become pregnant by "live cover"—mating with a stallion in the way that nature intended, just as if they were living wild on a prairie. In the Thoroughbred world, artificial insemination is not allowed, meaning that a mare cannot become pregnant in any other way than by directly being in contact with a stallion fertilizing an egg in her womb by live cover. This rule limits a stallion to being the sire to only about two hundred foals a year; whereas by artificial means, a stallion could father many more. This way, the population of Thoroughbreds is limited.

When a mare is pregnant, she is described as being *in foal*.

The year of 2012, when American Pharoah was born, thousands of other Thoroughbreds—colts and fillies— entered the world with the goal of a racing career. It turned out that the foal heat of his mother after his birth failed to "catch," meaning the egg in her womb was not fertilized; so she did not produce a foal in 2013. It was not until January 27, 2014, that she produced a full sister to Pharoah, a filly to be named American Cleopatra.

On February 13, 2015, Littleprincessemma would deliver a full brother to American Pharoah to be named Irish Pharaoh.

5

HARD GOOD-BYES

AT TWO AND a half months old, the brown colt with the floating walk, along with his mother, were loaded up in a trailer and moved to the Vinery. There, on this Kentucky farm of 440 acres near where he was born, and where his sire stood as a breeding stallion, the colt followed his mother off the trailer. Farm Manager Frances Relihan met Little-princessemma's colt. She spoke soothing words to him as she attached a tag to his halter that identified him by his mother's name. After Frances made sure the colt went safely with Littleprincessemma into the barn, she would now become the most important person in the young horse's life.

Frances had come from Listowel, Ireland, prompted by her dream of working with Thoroughbreds in the famous bluegrass country of Kentucky. Often she could be seen with her reddish-golden hair moving quickly around the farm, tending to the fifty-five foals in her care. She divided them into groups of eight, made up of mares with their foals. To one of these groups Littleprincessemma and her foal were assigned.

For the next three months, this group of other mares and foals would become their "herd," giving the foals a sense of safety and a social education. Discovering who was the boss mare, and who was the foal leader, taught the foals valuable lessons in confidence, as well as how to get along.

All the foals were Frances's delight, as well as the center of her days. She called them "her babies." While her joy in caring for them wrapped every minute of every day, her anxiety to keep them safe was like a worrisome drumbeat that never fell silent.

Every day, standing at the pasture fence, her eyes searched for any source of danger. The foals needed a lot of room for each to discover what they could do: to run, to outrun each other, to feel their desire to be in the lead, to plumb the depths of their courage, their grit, their joy. And there was always the chance that one little nail in the fence was sticking out somewhere. And more often than not, some foal would find it. Protecting them as they horse-wrestled in their herd was a never-ending job.

As she watched, she studied them, and wrote down her observations. Always, Littleprincessemma's colt caught her attention. There was something about his physical presence that fascinated her.

Even though most of the foals that his father, Pioneerof the Nile, had sired were outstanding, with great promise as racehorses, Littleprincessemma's colt stood out even more. He had a very athletic walk. As if his shoulder had an extra hinge, he reached out in a naturally long stride. He seemed to float as he moved. He was also very physically correct, with very good bone substance that looked hardy and substantial. Everyone who handled him reported that he had an exceptionally sweet temperament.

Whenever Frances walked in the pasture to look them over more closely, the gang of foals trotted forward to surround her like a fan club. She was their conduit to learning that humans could be trusted.

In her lilting Irish accent, she asked, "And how are you today, handsome boy? And you?" She would rub the forehead of Littleprincessemma's foal. "Any problems? Any complaints?"

What Frances dreaded was the process of weaning, which each foal would have to undergo at the age of five months. It was a hard thing to watch. Separating them from their mothers would be one of the most stressful events in their lives. Mares often ran and called when their foals were taken away. Their frantic whinnies were like siren calls to the separated baby, and foals called back in desperate high-pitched voices, wrung from their pinched hearts.

Some foals ran their stalls or paddocks, fretting. Some got so nervous they dropped a lot of weight. Some even hurt themselves in their desperation to reunite with their mothers. Their farewells echoed from the thousands of years that mothers and their young had realized that they each must live in the world on their own. It was a song of a thousand sorrows.

During the months that Frances Relihan watched over "her foals," they grew tall, gangly, rambunctious, and, above all, impetuous. Since it was now the middle of summer, their foal winter coats had shed to show slick, round bodies. Their baby teeth, which had erupted after they were one week old, had been added to, so that they now had twelve. They were learning to eat grain.

While Littleprincessemma's colt at a distance blended in with all the other bay colts, Frances could always pick him out. She decided she should call his owner in New Jersey to report on all the foals he had at the Vinery, as well as this special one she loved to watch. Since the foal's owner had some two hundred other Thoroughbreds, he stabled them around the country with various trainers in their barns at racetracks or at various farms for breeding and early training. Usually he kept thirty *broodmares*—the term for mares to be bred often—and their foals in Kentucky. He kept about twenty yearlings at other farms in preparation for training or selling. Here at the Vinery, he owned not only Littleprincessemma and her foal, but also his sire, Pioneerof the Nile.

When Frances called the colt's owner in New Jersey at his business office, she said, "I think you're going to be really pleased with Littleprincessemma's colt. Physically, he's the best foal on the farm . . . this could be a graded stakes horse."

Graded stakes, the highest caliber of races with the most competition—*that* was certainly an accurate prediction.

Yet before the colt could fulfill any promise, Frances Relihan had to get him safely through the weaning process.

She set her mind now to doing that.

On the chosen July evening when the mares and foals were turned out into their pasture to spend the night in the cool air, Frances clipped a lead onto Littleprincessemma's halter and led her out of the gate to take her to another pasture. The weaning had begun.

The bay colt raised his head and looked after his mother. She called back to him. He answered in a brief, high-pitched whinny. Maybe he assumed that in only a little while, she would return. By now he was bonded to his pasture buddies, even though they could never take the place of his mother. Being a part of the foal herd always provided comfort.

After another long look after her, he put his head down and continued to eat grass, surrounded by the other foals and their mothers.

Would he run and fret all night? Would he grow anxious and stop grazing when he discovered that his mother had not come back? When the sun came up the next morning, would he accept being led into a stall in the barn to be there all day, alone?

As Frances led away Littleprincessemma to another pasture, she glanced back and whispered, "Please, stay safe."

6

A MOVE TO THE FUTURE

IN 1989, TWENTY-THREE years before the colt was separated from his mother in Kentucky, seventeen-year-old Victor climbed on a bus in his hometown of Tulancingo in the state of Hidalgo, to move to Mexico City. He had just graduated from high school and had been living with his brother José in Cancún on a quarter-horse ranch. José had found work there. Leaving home to find work was usual in a world that offered so few ways to make a living.

It was there with José at that quarter-horse ranch in Cancún that Victor learned firsthand something of the nature of a horse—and that they terrified him.

Horses—their size, their catlike impetuous natures, and their daunting power—well, they could crush him in a blazing second. On the other hand, they were a perfect fit. When he was sixteen he had seen his first race, a quarter-horse race, which gave him ideas. Here he was, seventeen years old and no bigger than most twelve-year-olds. With no likelihood that he would grow bigger, he realized that being a jockey might be a realistic goal.

He was strong, wiry, and athletic. After all, what does a man do to be a man when up against those twice his size? Being a man meant making your own way in the world, being respected, being free.

To become a jockey would mean conquering his fears—of horses, of homesickness, of failure, of hunger. But money, money—there was always the need for it. How else to buy food, a place to stay, a way to keep his head above the bone-wearying poverty that lined the faces of so many he saw? Having no way to make a living was a nightmare that drove him awake with each sunrise.

He realized that he would have to learn to be brave.

Now he had come home to see his mother before he started on his new life plan. After saying good-bye, he climbed on the bus in Tulancingo with a lump of emotion swelling in his throat. He could soothe himself by saying over and over, *This doesn't mean you're leaving forever; this might be just for a little while, a little while, yes, a little while.* If he let himself realize that this farewell might be for a lifetime, his heart might feel so squeezed he would lose all courage.

As the bus pulled out of his hometown, he turned and

looked back with the lump throbbing in his throat. While traveling the fifty-seven miles to Mexico City, he struck up a conversation with anyone he met—especially if it was someone who owned a business. He plumbed their minds, asking how they put together the ingredients for success. What were their future plans? His curiosity about how to design a successful life for himself was bottomless and insatiable. *He would do this, yes, he would do this, he would.* It was as if being successful were a promise he was making to himself.

In Mexico City he moved in with his sister and signed up for jockey school. Becoming a licensed jockey would take him a year, depending on how much time he could give to attending classes and riding horses. After all, he had to find a part-time job to pay his tuition and support himself. Within a couple of days, he found a job—the perfect one, if not the safest. He was hired to drive a bus.

In jockey school his first lessons started with grooming horses, watering and feeding them, and learning about their natures. Certainly there were things about them he had never imagined. There were constant dangers. Getting stepped on was number one. Being calm but quick on his feet became a habit—when leading them, grooming them, walking around them. He learned to always lead and mount a horse on its left side—a holdover from days when soldiers mounted with a sword carried on *their* left side.

Because of horses' funny eyesight, he became keenly aware of their blind spots. With their eyes placed on the sides of their heads, they have a 350-degree range of vision. While this peripheral vision allows them to see a predator sneaking up, the position of their eyes also means that there's a blind spot in front of the forehead, and another one right behind the tail. Woe to anyone accidentally getting in one of these blind spots and setting off a defense, such as a striking front hoof or a kick.

As "flight" animals, their unusual eyesight is constantly on call, ready to enact their number one defense—running. Their eyes are the largest of any land animal, and unlike humans, they have a third eyelid, which is a membrane resting in the corner of their eye that can draw somewhat like a curtain diagonally over the cornea to protect the lens.

So when opening a stall door to go in, Victor always made sure a horse saw him. Along with zebras and donkeys, horses are the only ungulates—hoofed mammals—that can sleep standing up. They can look awake even when they aren't. In their stifles—the part of their anatomy in their back legs analogous to a human's knee—ligaments lock to keep them standing while asleep, so they are always ready to run. But if cornered, they can kick, bite, stomp, and, as a last resort, mash their heavy bodies against their enemy to crush it against something immovable, like a wall. All of this was trouble Victor planned never to get into.

So opening a stall door and going in, Victor adopted the habit of chattering, saying something playful, like calling them best friend, "*Ah, mejor amigo.*" Or announcing dinner: "*Estamos cenando.*"

In the process of understanding them, he found he had a natural, quiet way that gained their trust. His fear of them became less with his knowledge. But he also realized another danger. Always, he'd had a quick affection for any animal, dogs especially. Now he found that he could not complicate his job as a jockey by opening his heart to one horse or another. Becoming attached to any would get in his way. This was a *business*. This was to be his job. He was in training.

When he was riding one out on a track, learning the way a jockey's positions could communicate with a horse, he had to protect himself, not just with a helmet and padded vest, but emotionally. He had to always move quickly from one horse to another, and never look back. *Keep going, always going.*

Like many jockeys, he ate very little, often only tea and toast, to keep his weight light. Knowing that he could never outmuscle a horse, he relied on outthinking them, avoiding trouble, and staying fit so as not to hamper them by his own lack of balance. He did leg stretches and built up his stamina.

Riding different ones with different personalities and different needs, he discovered something else. Not only was he the right size, and the right strength, he also had something unusual—perhaps close to magic—in his hands. With his hands holding the thick racing reins, he discovered he could squeeze his fingers to send different messages through the line of reins connected to the bit in the horse's mouth. Control the head of a horse, and its body will follow.

Using his wrists as if they were elastic bands, he was in constant contact with the horse's mouth, which in a sense was its communications headquarters. As if he were holding baby birds in his hands, he could squeeze his fingers on the reins to produce a light, elastic touch that horses seemed to immediately trust. And they would relax. Their heads would go down, their bodies would loosen, and they would flow from the shoulder with no jarring stiffness.

He knew how to help balance their big, heavy bodies

with the reins, much like a ballet dancer balancing against a ballet barre or a partner's hand. He could urge them by sending feverish messages through the reins to *run, run, tap the speed engine, seek the lead.*

Earning money to pay his tuition and his living expenses took a lot of time, but ironically, his job of driving a bus was a gift. If not the safest, it was actually the perfect job to put the finishing touch on becoming a winning jockey. For driving a bus in Mexico City was like jumping into a food mixer and dodging the blades. It took guts, savvy, a bit of a daredevil flair, as well as luck.

Amid the smell of gas fumes with the sound of screeching brakes, Victor dealt with potholes, a lack of signs, seven-way intersections, confusing traffic circles, tamale vendors on tricycles, and cops thirsty to ticket for easy money. He learned to thread the bus through clogged traffic, and to gun to an open lane.

No, there could not have been a better training ground for a jockey—although he did not realize it. Mexico City traffic was ten times more dangerous than riding a Thoroughbred at racing speed. In Mexico City traffic, a motorist was killed or injured every hour.

With all this training, by 1990 Victor was racing

Thoroughbreds at Mexico City's track, the Hipódromo de las Américas, winning at least a fair share of the time. Driving the bus became history.

Now, every so often, a foreign jockey would catch his eye. As he rode his own assigned horse, he would glance over. He would study the other jockeys' positions, their way of riding. There was something about them that was different. When he asked, he was told that these jockeys whom he admired were Americans—Americans who had come down from California to get work as jockeys at the Mexico City track.

There was something about them that he wanted for himself. The word *elegante* came to his mind. Yes, that was a way to describe what he saw. *They are elegant.* Elegant in the way they sat, the way they rode, the way they won.

The idea of going to America began tickling his mind.

7

PEAKS AND VALLEYS

ON THE JULY 2012 morning in Kentucky after Frances Relihan began weaning the bay colt with the floating walk and sweet nature, she went to the pasture where he had spent his first night without his mother. Frances opened the gate and took a deep breath. Willingly, calmly, the colt came to her. When she slipped a lead rope through his halter, he followed her with a skip and a high-headed playfulness.

She led him to his old stall in Barn 9, which he had occupied with his mother. When Frances opened the sliding stall door and led him in, the colt was calm and accepting. Then she left him there alone. His mother was now in another part of the farm.

Throughout the morning, Frances checked on him. The young horse looked out of his stall quietly, stoic in his acceptance that his mother was no longer with him. His eye was soft; his demeanor composed. He was like a model for the other foals, all of them now called *weanlings.*

Quickly, he adjusted to this new stage in his life. Just as quickly, an inner confidence began swelling inside him, giving him a majestic air. Even though he was still very young, he began to have a way about him, a presence that was singular. He could now catch any mere human's eye. He looked out at the world with bold self-assurance.

Down through history there have been many stories about horses with that bearing. One of the most famous story-horses, Pegasus, had wings, which led him to play a leading role in a list of myths that have traveled down through time. In his first appearance, Pegasus pawed the earth, and a spring flowed forth. Here, too, in this story of the unnamed brown colt with the floating walk and sweet nature, there would be a moment when he would touch earth and wishes and longings would spring forth, all promising to come true.

Certainly, lives would be changed.

In the summer of 1984, thirty-eight years before the bay colt was weaned, a twelve-year-old boy named Ahmed Zayat rode his jumping horse in a show in Cairo, Egypt. He was about to live out an old story, one familiar to many kids who engage in the sport of show jumping. One step from a jump, one step from becoming airborne, his horse suddenly stuck its hooves in the ground and stopped. The boy went sailing over the head of the horse and even over the jump, landing on the ground.

He lay sprawled in the dirt. After catching his breath, he discovered that nothing was hurt but his pride. He sat up and looked at the horse, which wore no look of apology.

In show jumping, there is a saying that a horse can "stop dirty," meaning it gives no signals that it is about to refuse to jump a fence. That was what happened this time—as it happens every year to any number of kids who ride horses over jumps. Accepting the prospect of a sudden turn and a hard disappointment is part of this sport.

By then, Ahmed Zayat knew—just as all kids learn—that having a relationship with a horse requires constant renegotiation. As a herd animal, a horse always prefers a horse buddy to a human friend. Maybe that's why having a relationship with a horse is good training for other relationships in life: you can't take the partnership for granted.

As Ahmed Zayat sat in the dirt, nursing his bruise from landing, he had choices: walk off, get back on to show his courage, get back on and jump the round to look like a man.

SHELLEY FRASER MICKLE

Or he could get up, calmly look over the horse for signs of an injury, and then get back on, motivated by something so very hard to describe.

◾ AN INEXPLICABLE PASSION ◾

Many writers over many years have tried to capture this relationship between humans and horses, driven by something so very hard to describe. It might be appropriately termed "a calling." And that calling most often happens to two-legged humans when they are young.

Possibly the best description of such a bond can be found in the classic 1941 novel *My Friend Flicka*, when Ken, the main character, chooses a yearling from a herd to be his own: "No dream he had ever had, no imagination of adventure or triumph could touch this moment. He felt as if he had burst out of his old self and was something entirely new—and that the world had burst into something new too. So this was it—this was what being alive meant—Oh, my filly, my filly, my beautiful—"

As Ken discovers a depth to love that he has not experienced before, he is changed. For sure, mystery gives voice to the calling, since only certain people hear it. The list of those who do is both fascinating and sometimes unexpected. President Ronald Reagan heard it. President Lincoln and General Ulysses S. Grant heard it. Cormac McCarthy, the esteemed American writer, described it when he wrote about one of his characters that his attraction to horses, "the ardenthearted," came from his love of "the blood and the heat of the blood that ran them."

President Ronald Reagan, as a young athlete with the dream of becoming a star football player, discovered that on a football field he relished the animalistic head-to-head combat of one man against another playing on the line. On the day he realized that a horse possesses more muscle power in its neck than he, as a man, could count in his whole body, he was disarmed by admiration. And hooked. Later, as president, when he had some momentous decision to make, he took to the back of a horse to ride the trails, where he said he did his clearest thinking.

In the last bloody days of the Civil War, President Lincoln, whom we don't think of as a rider, made almost daily journeys to meet General Ulysses Grant so they could take turns riding General Grant's favorite horses, Cincinnati and Egypt. Grant would allow no one else to ride them, but these two men—battered leaders in the agonizing conflict that saved America as one nation—found a bit of serenity through their shared admiration for the magnificent Egypt and the steadfast Cincinnati.

We absorb these moments as they bridge the divide between the species of man and horse, rarely taking notice. And we pass down words that struggle to capture it.

"A horse! a horse! My kingdom for a horse!" Who does not at some time commit this line from Shakespeare to memory?

"The outside of a horse is good for the inside of a man," said often and attributed to both Winston Churchill, who led Britain through World War II, and American humorist Will Rogers.

Jumping from reality to fantasy, we accept in our

stories the unicorn and the centaur with nary a hitch of disbelief.

The list goes on and on . . . as again and again, decade after decade, the inexplicable passion whispers to a child, and the calling is heard.

So the young boy in Egypt, Ahmed Zayat, who show-jumped horses and fell off thirty-eight years before Little-princessemma's colt was weaned, carried his lifelong love of horses. He planned to mix it with whatever else he chose to be in his life—be it a banker, an engineer, a teacher, a baker, a candlestick maker. . . . He blended his passion for horses with his competitive nature to vow that one day he would own a string of Thoroughbreds.

But until then, he had to find his way. In Cairo, Ahmed Zayat led a charmed life. He had wealthy parents and a famous family.

His grandfather was an esteemed writer in Egypt. His father was a prominent physician, even the physician to the Egyptian president, Anwar Sadat. Ahmed's family was part of a small community of Jewish Egyptians. When President Sadat was assassinated in 1981, the political unrest prompted Ahmed Zayat to emigrate to the United States to attend college. He earned a bachelor's degree at Yeshiva University and a master's degree at Boston University.

He then returned to Egypt to become the businessman he had set out to be, which was really a means to fund his dream of owning a stable of exceptional Thoroughbreds. He succeeded by developing a nonalcoholic drink that became so popular in Egypt that he earned millions by selling it to an international company. He was on his way, and America was where it would all happen, he was certain. By then, he was part of the last generation of Jews in Egypt, which would soon nearly vanish.

His quest for freedom brought him back to the United States. With an immigrant's optimism, he took up chasing his dream with unabashed zeal, as if he were taking a bite of life and letting it dribble down his chin.

By 2005, he had established his stable of competitive Thoroughbreds. One of his first purchases was a horse he wanted to name Maimonides, after the Jewish philosopher, respected by both Jews and Muslims. Zayat explained, "If this horse was going to be a superstar, I wanted an appropriate name. . . . I wanted it to be pro-peace, and about loving your neighbor." Since the name had already been reserved by another racehorse owner, Zayat made a deal with that owner to release the name.

In the first of many frustrations, his horse Maimonides

ran two races and then had to be retired with an injury. It would be another whole year before Ahmed Zayat's heavy investments in buying promising young Thoroughbreds began paying off. In three Kentucky Derbies between 2009 and 2013, his horses came in second.

In 2009 Pioneerof the Nile was second in the Derby. The following year, Zayat's horse Eskendereya was a heavy favorite to win but was scratched before the Derby with a career-ending injury. In 2011 his horse Nehro finished second in the Derby, as did Bodemeister in 2012. But it was his horse Paynter that earned Zayat the admiration of fans beyond wins, as well as put his passion for horses on public display.

After Paynter ran second in the Belmont, and then won the Haskell Invitational, he developed life-threatening health problems. He was dying of colitis, losing hundreds of pounds, and also developed laminitis—the disease that had caused another famous Thoroughbred colt, Barbaro, to be euthanized years before—in three hooves. Zayat spared no expense saving Paynter's life, even turning to social media—with a hashtag of #powerupPaynter—to put out daily updates on the horse's condition.

Kids and fans sent get-well cards to Paynter and followed

him as he recovered. Miraculously, the horse went on to run three more graded stakes races, finishing second in two of them. After he courageously ran seventh in the Breeders' Cup Classic, he was retired as a breeding stallion in Kentucky in 2014.

As Ahmed Zayat quickly ascended to the top of horse racing, he also became a well-known owner in the "Sport of Kings." With his main residence in Teaneck, New Jersey, he traveled from track to track with his wife and four children, often parking a camper near the track so he could observe Orthodox Jewish kosher laws regarding food, which involved fixing his own meals.

Identifying himself as both Jewish and Muslim, he quickly answered when asked about his religious affiliations, "Why is it relevant, and why does it matter? It's personal."

After nine years of being in the horse-racing business, Zayat and his son Justin, who began to help run Zayat Stables, knew that with horses, as with living, there are peaks and valleys to be climbed and endured. Yet he had done what he had set out to do: he had accomplished his dream of owning a stable of outstanding Thoroughbreds.

Sailing on the eternal hopes of winning in horse racing, he purchased a yearling filly in 2007 that he named

Littleprincessemma. He bred her to his stallion Pioneerof the Nile.

We all know what came of that.

Yes, the unnamed brown colt with the floating walk and sweet nature was his. But with business expenses, there was always the challenge of balancing the columns of money in and money out. As the year turned to 2013, Ahmed Zayat had debts. Hearing Frances Relihan's prediction that Littleprincessemma's foal would be valuable was good news indeed. At one time Zayat had even considered selling Littleprincessemma while she was in foal with the little brown colt.

Now, in the process of juggling his inventory of horses, he made the hard decision to sell the unnamed brown colt as a yearling.

Littleprincessemma's colt's future would soon be up for grabs.

8

GETTING READY FOR THE AUCTION BLOCK

FOR AN ADDITIONAL six months as a weanling, Little-princessemma's colt stayed at the Vinery in Kentucky, growing and playing in the big green pastures with his horse buddies. That January of 2013, his official racehorse birthday declared him a yearling.

Since Ahmed Zayat had plans to sell him, he was loaded up in late January and driven to Taylor Made Farm outside Lexington, Kentucky. At any given time, Taylor Made Farm was home to five hundred horses, among them 120 yearlings. Now Littleprincessemma's yearling would be prepared to be put up for auction.

Being sent so many places as a young colt gave him an inadvertent benefit: he became adaptable, a trait that later would become very valuable to a winning racehorse. Since Zayat owned the stallion Pioneerof the Nile, the brown colt, as a son of this sire, would now be a great advertisement for this bloodline. So the unnamed bay colt with the regal bearing was destined for the auction block at the Saratoga, New York, sales that next summer.

Those first days at the Taylor Made Farm, Mark Taylor, vice president of marketing and public sales, who'd seen many good horses, noticed Littleprincessemma's colt had that "it" factor. Frank Taylor remarked, "If you're around a lot of very good horses, they have an air or presence about them. Like they'll prick their ears and just look way off in the distance. [American Pharoah] did that early on, had a lot of class. He just had it all. . . . And he's really smart."

John Hall, the yearling manager, assigned the colt to a group of eight other yearlings to spend the day in a large pasture where they had room to exercise and play. Every morning the colt was brought into the barn to be fed and groomed, and was then turned back out to spend the day in the gentle sun and to graze on the winter grass.

Cesar Terrazas, the division manager for the yearlings, assigned Mauro Lucas to groom and handle the colt. Each time Mauro led the colt or worked around him, he discovered that Littleprincessemma's yearling was very mentally mature and obedient. Already, the colt's sweet temperament had been stamped with lessons of trust that would never forsake him.

For those other yearlings, who were not so mature or mentally ready to cooperate, the farm used the Monty Roberts method of communicating, a method that some call "horse whispering." Since Littleprincessemma's yearling already trusted humans and had a natural willingness to cooperate, he was simply hand-walked and handled every day by Mauro or another employee under Cesar and John Hall's supervision.

Mark Taylor agreed with what John Hall noted about Pharoah, that "The colt was almost like an old soul; everything you introduced him to he just didn't really turn a hair. It was like he had been doing it his whole life."

In early May, as the sun gained its summer strength, the yearlings were taken into the barn for the day to keep their coats from becoming faded and dried. Then they were turned out at night when the air was cool.

As the August auction in Saratoga drew near, the brown colt's schedule changed.

For six weeks, each day he was hand-walked for forty-five minutes. He then spent the rest of the day in his stall in the barn, until seven in the evening. He was now turned out in a paddock alone so he wouldn't be likely to get nicks and scrapes playing with other yearlings.

With the daily grooming, his coat took on the sheen and gloss of hot fudge. Each day, his combs and brushes were washed to prevent skin disease. He was fed a high-protein sweet feed with a dollop of oil added for even more sheen. While he was groomed, a thick-ring chifney bit was put in his mouth. This chifney would get him used to having a racing *snaffle* later. But for now it would be used to display all the yearlings in the auction ring, since it gave the handler control. Similar to a choke collar on a dog, the chifney could apply pressure to capture a young animal's attention, if he was about to do something that could result in an injury. Above all, the safety of these valuable young horses was on everyone's mind.

And yet it happened, as it can always happen to a young horse—Littleprincessemma's colt banged his right front ankle a month before the sale. No one knew how it happened. But there was a small swelling just above his hoof. With a racehorse's legs comparable to the winning parts of a race car, this bump would put off potential buyers.

The mystery of how it happened would never be solved. He could have gotten cast in his stall, which is something that happens when a horse lies down too close to the wall with no room to stretch out its legs to get up, so it thrashes about, trying to stand, and sometimes gets banged up while doing so. The swelling was not connected to a structural part—bone or soft tissue—but it was there all the same. And then his tail—oh, his tail!

It simply disappeared one day, half chewed off. Who did the chewing, no yearling would admit. Only the top of the tail was left, with one long string, like a spaghetti noodle, hanging down.

The crime of stealing the tail from the promising yearling could never be pinned on any living creature. It was August, with the sale only days away. Would he have to appear in public that way?

He didn't care. All he missed was the diminished power of his flyswatter.

◣ THE ART OF HORSE WHISPERING ◢

Since yearlings shown at auction have to have good manners, the Taylor Made farm staff are adept at using a method that some call "horse whispering," that is, talking to a young horse in his own "Equus language," as explained in the book *The Man Who Listens to Horses*, written by horseman Monty Roberts.

In this method, any horse, especially a young

one, is taken frequently to a round pen to be "spoken to" in his own language. Being a prey animal that naturally wants to run in a herd, a horse is hardwired to turn over leadership to an alpha horse who will guide him. At Taylor Made Farm, the covered round pen is a circle with a sixty-foot diameter, where each day a yearling is made to trot in both directions for ten to twenty minutes. Not only does this make the yearlings fit, the instinct of horses to give themselves to a leader can be transferred to a human by using certain body language. Through the movements the trainer makes, the horse will instinctively understand.

As the yearling is trotting in the round-pen circle to the right, his direction is suddenly changed by the trainer blocking his path. So the young horse turns and trots in the circle to the left.

Changing the horse's direction in the round pen convinces him that the person making him change is the one in charge, and can be trusted. Mentally, the horse begins to defer to the human calling the shots. In this deference he will soon "join up," which is the moment the trainer is looking for. "Join up" is the term horse whisperers use for the moment the horse talks back to him by signaling a desire to follow.

Monty Roberts even identified a horse's fear response to certain signals, such as spreading fingers to simulate a bear claw. The horse, thinking he sees what could be a bear, will run faster in the round pen. Close your fingers, step back, lower your head below the horse's head, and the horse will think the threat is over and will slow down. In short, whenever the human trainer advances toward the trotting yearling, he will go faster. When the human trainer retreats, the young untrained horse will slow down.

While the trainer is speaking this language to a horse, he is studying the young horse's inside ear closest to him as he stands in the center of the round pen. After a few minutes, that ear will stop moving as it begins to "listen" to the human speaking in his language. The outside ear, however, still moves as it continues to monitor his surroundings. Soon the young horse will tip his head. His neck will bend slightly toward the human in the center of the circle. And now the young horse begins licking and chewing, running his tongue around his mouth—a signal the trainer is looking for.

As the young horse lowers his head near the ground, Monty Roberts says the horse is sending a message to the human as if saying, *Hey, look! I am a flight animal, and I'm eating so I can't fear you. If we could have a meeting to renegotiate, I would let you be the boss.* The horse's behavior is asking the trainer to take the pressure off and let him stop trotting around, going nowhere.

Now the trainer must be careful not to challenge the young horse by looking into his eyes. Instead, the trainer brings his shoulder to a forty-five-degree position in an invitation for the young horse to stop retreating. Now the young horse will "join up" by walking toward the trainer calmly and submissively as if saying, *Okay, you are my leader; I trust you. So what now?*

When a young horse accepts the trainer as his leader, he will willingly follow anyone he gives that power to. Sometimes he will even follow the human without halter and lead. And for the rest of his life, the young horse is likely to transfer that willingness to another human as his leader—unless something unfortunate happens to make him lose that trust.

The bond between a horse and the person who gains his trust can last a lifetime.

9

STILL ON THE MOVE

IN 1992, TWENTY-ONE YEARS before the brown colt was put up for auction, Victor Espinoza got on a plane with his brother José to fly from Mexico City to San Francisco, California. José was already working there at the nearby Bay Meadows racetrack. Victor was now nearly twenty years old.

Right after they landed, they took a bus into town to José's apartment across from the track. There Victor froze, looking around at his strange surroundings—the city traffic, the noise, the sounds of English being spoken everywhere, so foreign to him. He turned to his brother and said, "You want me to live here?"

José looked back at him, baffled. "Yeah."

Victor swallowed, thinking, *Man, I'm miserable. I mean I can't even talk.* He went outside, shaking. His brother suggested they go for a cup of hot chocolate. In a couple of hours, Victor was calm enough to accept that he was now in a whole new world—one that would challenge him to the utmost.

Right off, Victor set out to learn English. He watched only American programs on television every moment he could, inhaling the use of English. He concentrated so hard on learning this new language that he spent little time doing anything else.

He was definitely in the right place to chase his goal of becoming a professional jockey. California is a horse-racing hub, with some fourteen racecourses. Among them were Santa Anita Park in Los Angeles County and the famous Del Mar Racetrack in San Diego. Del Mar was especially famous, established in 1937 by singer and movie star Bing Crosby. It was also the track where the legendary horse Seabiscuit won his most famous race.

Right off, Victor became a licensed apprentice jockey. With that job, he earned the papers that gave him the legal right to work and live in America. He moved out of his brother's apartment and slept in the tack room, not only to save money but to also constantly be around the trainers who might hire him. Furthermore, his brother José had his own life and would eventually marry and have two children.

During those years of being an apprentice jockey, Victor hardly ever left the track. He had to constantly be ready to entice trainers to let him gallop horses in the early-morning workouts, which could lead to gaining mounts to race later in the day. Always, he could find a place to sleep in a tack room or empty stall, but with no money in his pocket, he could not eat. The fear of poverty had moved with him. Now it woke up with him each daybreak as the racetrack life began—the sound of footsteps in the barns, horses neighing, feed buckets clanging, the swoosh of water filling buckets, the chatter of trainers and exercise riders heading to the track for workouts in the dark.

All the while, loneliness and fear of failure coursed through his thoughts like a hidden illness. Only being busy relieved the misery of homesickness.

Soon he became known as that hardworking kid who was always around. Yet sometimes he fantasized that someone would come barging in, telling him he had no right to be in America and to go home. Then he'd jump up, relieved of his fear of failure, and head home like a stray pup, exhausted by freedom.

His perseverance was always threatened by a sabotage dragon lying in wait, whispering, *Give up, give up, give up.*

In the program for the daily races, an asterisk appeared beside his name, identifying him as a licensed apprentice jockey, also known as a "bug." It was always hard to get a mount. Convincing a trainer to let him ride was not easy, especially when the English words he knew were mostly those of a TV host on a game show.

The ups and downs were like the motion of a carousel—one win, three losses, no mount, no trainers calling. The profession was a chillingly tough one. There was the constant threat of life-altering injuries—concussions, bone fractures, and paralysis. No wonder a jockey's insurance premiums are the highest of all professional sports.

Always, too, there was that unforgiving requirement to make the weight. Racing authorities set the amounts that jockeys could weigh, with the Super Bowl–like Kentucky Derby having a limit of only 126 pounds, *including* the saddle. Maintaining the strength to control a twelve-hundred-pound Thoroughbred going forty miles an hour kept Victor in the gym and on daily five-mile runs. He worked hard, doing everything he could to be in tip-top condition. He ate well, never drank alcohol, and put his career above everything.

He won his first race in 1993 on a horse named X-Rays—

which he thought was a funny name. And then, it was a real disappointment when he went the next three months without a win. "I feel like quitting now," he admitted to himself. Here he had been riding four or five horses a day, and he couldn't win a race.

Then, later that year, the wins finally started coming. Word got around: success built on success, and more offers to ride good horses came his way.

By 1994, Victor was the leading apprentice rider at the Bay Meadows track. As a California apprentice rider, he became a professional jockey one year from the date of his fifth winning ride in 1995. He then got an agent, who was responsible for getting him rides on good horses by contacting trainers and working through a network of people at racetracks.

One day he was on a horse that wouldn't listen to him at all—not to any of his cues, his riding signals, the reins, or his voice. He had no way to control it. Victor held on for dear life. Then he became furious at himself for being terrified.

The next day he joined a gym to add more strenuous workouts. He toned and strengthened his muscles until they were like a collection of coiled wire cables. Knowing how strong he was now gave him comfort. He felt equal to anything a horse might try. In a sense, he became as cool as if ice water flowed in his veins. In a sense, too, he walked toward his fear and made a friend of it.

He reminded himself that horses were living beings just like he was; they might wake up on any given day and decide they didn't want to run. They could be in a bad mood or tired. He couldn't always completely control them, and that was okay. He had enough skill and strength to distract them, to coax them to do what had to be done.

In 1995 Victor moved his riding gear to Los Angeles. Five years later he had his breakout year, in which he won three major titles: the Breeders' Cup Distaff, the Hollywood Gold Cup, and the Del Mar Mile Handicap. He also won fifteen graded stakes races.

He rode his first Kentucky Derby in 2001, placing third on Congaree. The following year he won both the Kentucky Derby and the Preakness Stakes atop War Emblem. He'd even had a chance at the Triple Crown with War Emblem, until that disastrous stumble out of the starting gate. He was averaging 193 wins a year and twice finished third in total earnings among jockeys.

But suddenly his career stuck its heels in the dirt and

threw him into a slump. What was this? How ironic and cruel that just as he was achieving success, success refused to be what he could count on. Here he was again in a place with a new set of challenges—unexpected and unpredicted. The rhythm of life clearly had its own beat that he would have to adjust to.

He learned that perception was everything. Even though he was now thirty years old, many trainers still thought of him as the kid who had trouble getting a mount. In a sport in which winning was everything, measured in terms of dollars from each race, his numbers followed him like a shadow. It was a sport where attachments were few; loyalty was as rare as hen's teeth. The daily grind was getting to him.

Even with wins, the money totals of the races in which he either won or placed didn't get him attention from the trainers who had the top-notch horses—the ones running in the Triple Crown races. Finishing a race out of the money became the monster always breathing down his neck. As he remarked to a friend, "It was a little bit easy for me to get to the top. But when you go down, you drop like a ball in no time."

However, could these explanations reflect less than the

whole truth? He wondered: might there be deeper reasons that he had to face? Sure, he was riding in races every week. But his yearly earnings were half of what he'd brought in before. Back in 2002 when War Emblem had stumbled out of the gate in a chance for a Triple Crown, had Victor's heart gone down with him? With that failure, Victor felt he'd disappointed everyone: the owner, the trainer, and, most of all, the crowd that had come to see a Triple Crown winner and instead had watched Victor and War Emblem struggle to the finish line.

It seemed as if for over ten years, Victor had been riding in a fog, going from one race to another without his heart really being in the game. Was he afraid of failing, afraid of disappointing himself and so many others? Was it that, coupled with the pressure, the daily grind, the need for energy, the constant call for courage? Well, then . . . with this hard look at himself, he one day woke up and said, "This is not how I'm going to end up my career."

He hired a new agent.

He also learned to put life in perspective. A friend took him to a children's hospital, where he saw four- and five-year-olds battling diseases that threatened to steal their lives when they had barely begun living. Those children's bravery, their joy, their simple wish to live affected Victor so strongly that he rushed from the hospital and sat in the car to compose himself. From then on, he began donating a share of his earnings to the hospital.

In the summer of 2013, at the Del Mar Racetrack, a horse named California Chrome caught Victor's eye. The horse was two years old. Victor later said, "The second time I saw him run, I was, like, 'Wow, there's something about him that attracts me.' He seemed, like, really light on his feet when he was running."

Victor told his agent of his interest in the chestnut colt, and the message was sent through channels between trainers. After several months, Victor got a call: it was the offer to ride California Chrome.

Together, he and the chestnut colt produced four victories in four starts in California: the King Glorious Stakes, The California Cup Derby, the San Felipe Stakes, and the Santa Anita Derby. Then they headed to the 2014 Kentucky Derby in Louisville, which they won. Victor thought surely easy sailing was ahead. When he and California Chrome went on to win the Preakness, the future looked golden. The Triple Crown was missed by only inches when California Chrome faded in the stretch of the grueling Belmont and finished a gallant fourth.

How strange it seemed when after all this success, the phone didn't ring with riding offers. It was unbelievable. It didn't make sense; but clearly, the slump was here again. Simply, all the best horses already had jockeys assigned to them.

His agent wasn't able to get him rides on any of the upcoming stars either.

While Victor was chewing on this baffling situation, Littleprincessemma's colt was growing, maturing, guarding his secret of a speed song humming deep in his muscles, bones, and heart.

Soon, the yet unnamed brown colt with the floating walk and sweet temperament would touch Victor's life with the dust of a real-life fairy tale.

10

GOING ONCE, GOING TWICE, GOING NOT AT ALL

ON AN AUGUST evening in 2013, Littleprincessemma's colt followed the human who was leading him into the sale ring in Saratoga, New York. His hooves were polished, his coat was gleaming, and the human leading him was wearing a fancy black suit with white gloves. The colt himself wore a fake tail, a curious bump on his right ankle, and a number on his hip calling him *85*. Ahmed Zayat set the sale price at one million dollars.

Zayat was out of town with his family at the moment. He had assigned an agent to be at the auction in his place and was in touch by phone.

The breeding of Littleprincessemma's yearling was his calling card. He strutted it as if he were already a famous sports figure. Those in the auction audience studied their programs: Pioneerof the Nile, Littleprincessemma, Empire Maker, Unbridled, Storm Cat, Northern Dancer, even Secretariat on his mother's side. There were enough racehorse rock stars in his pedigree to produce a tongue twister—as well as the expected sale price of a million dollars.

The colt with hip number *85* carried a part of all who had gone before him. In every cell in his body, his DNA had two sets of instructions twisted together like a rope—one from his mother, the other from his father. These messages of life had been delivered by chromosomes, which acted like pens writing on every part of him as he was developing in Littleprincessemma's womb.

The thousands of genes in his chromosomes instructed him how to resemble his mother, his father, his grandparents—all the way back for many generations. Sometimes they told him how to be different. The way they blended made him who he was, uniquely—his temperament, his color, his bone structure, every part of him. So now he stood there as the fine offspring of many, yet holding a secret of a feverish love of speed that he would tell only when he was ready.

That love of speed had been nurtured from a distant

time, because the Thoroughbred breed was developed from only three stallions in the 1700s. At that time in the Mideast, three stallions became famous for their speed in the desert. When three Englishmen saw them, they fell in love with the stallions' unique traits, purchased them, and moved them to England.

There the three stallions were bred to stronger horses, so that traits of speed and endurance were passed on. The bay colt shared this lineage with all Thoroughbreds from their ancestral grandfathers: the Darley Arabian, the Godolphin Barb, and the Byerley Turk, named for their owners, Thomas Darley, Lord Francis Godolphin, and Captain Robert Byerley.

In the grand scheme of things, the bay colt represented an even more fascinating ancestry. Fossils were the storytellers that scientists followed to learn of horses' first appearance on earth, when they were the size of foxes in the Eocene epoch. This prehistoric horse, eohippus, had four toes on its forefeet and three on its hind feet. As Eohippus evolved to be tall enough to eat leaves and grasses so as not to compete for food with smaller animals, its toes receded.

As a modern horse, the bay colt carried this ancient

ancestry. Traces of the nonfunctioning second and fourth toes could be seen as vestigial splints on either side of his forefeet above the hoof. These splint bones are often banged in horseplay or when a leg accidentally strikes one, causing a swelling—which usually produces no serious consequences. While it was determined that the bump on Littleprincessemma's colt's leg was not a splint injury, no diagnosis could ever be made.

But the blemish was there. And it was putting bidders off. Ahmed Zayat's agent was at the sale, relaying information to Zayat by phone. As the bids went only haltingly up and that troubling news was sent to Zayat, the owner had shivers of doubt. "Why am I putting this horse here?" he asked himself. "If I'm not getting the kind of reception that we thought we would, I'm taking him home." He then instructed his agent to bid on the colt for *him*, which in a sense was a way to buy him back, or at least prevent anyone else from buying him for less than a million dollars.

One hundred thousand, two hundred thousand, three hundred thousand, the auctioneer rattled off. Then the bidders grew silent. The auctioneer waited. Finally he warned loudly: *Going once, going twice, sold for three hundred thousand dollars.* He banged his gavel.

It seemed strange that Ahmed Zayat had bought back his own colt. But it seemed the right thing to do.

Also, without really knowing it, he had dodged making a huge mistake.

11

"MAN, THAT'S TOO FAST!"

SINCE THE COLT was still a member of the Zayat Stables, he was sent to the McKathan Brothers training farm in Citra, Florida, near Ocala, to learn to be the racehorse he was born to be. He arrived on a horse van on a September morning just after sunrise. In only four months he would have his official second birthday.

Citra and Ocala, Florida, like Lexington and Louisville in Kentucky, have a natural environment where horses thrive. Limestone under the ground feeds the grass and water with the minerals to strengthen foals' bones. Furthermore, in Florida, sunshine assures continuous days for training. The weather is so constant that seasons most resemble a single song simply changing keys from spring to summer to fall to winter.

As Zayat's yearling colt was led off the van, he stopped

and looked. Wherever he was, he always liked to stop and look. The human leading him honored this personality trait by waiting patiently as the young horse looked over his surroundings. A light fog veiled the two hundred acres with beams of sun rays streaming through the foliage of oak trees. Birdsong drifted in the air, as if a chorus had shown up to sing background music for the young Thoroughbred's walk from the van.

The colt was led into the barn area, where farm manager Chris Alexander checked him in as *Littleprincessemma's colt*. Chris's daughter was a competitor on a college equestrian team. Horses were in his blood; caring for them was not just a job. He noted the exquisite horseflesh parading before him into a waiting stall.

The young Thoroughbred passed through a white plastic gate and down a covered walkway, known as a shedrow. Here, stalls opened onto the walkway so that horses in their stalls looked out, watching the newcomers come in.

Everything on the farm was designed by owners J. B. and Kevin McKathan with young horses' safety in mind. Certainly here, each young horse was treated like royalty.

In a sense they *were* royal. Several Kentucky Derby winners had been trained here, as well as many graded stakes horses. No one knew which would prove to be a winner. But while they were here to be "broken"—which is the horseman's term for putting a saddle and bridle on them and teaching them to gallop properly, how to conserve speed, how to summon speed on demand and go into a starting gate—each was regarded as a winner. Each held the promise of his own future.

Above all, they were to be protected with a staff of twenty horsemen trained for any emergency. At any given time, 100 to 120 young horses were being trained here. So the days were carefully orchestrated. If a horse got loose, a cry went out across the farm: *"Cierra la puerta.* Shut the gate!" And the main gate to the shedrow barns was quickly closed.

As soon as the bay colt looked over his new home, he was led to the first stall of the second barn, near the space between the two barns where J. B. and Kevin McKathan often sat to make plans for the day and to supervise training. No doubt the sound of human voices, with their chatter and laughter, drifted back to the colt. With his curious nature, he most likely relished the closeness of humans who gathered there at times throughout the day. Their sounds must have been comforting and a hedge against boredom.

Since a young horse finds that being groomed is sooth-ing, the bay colt was fed, curried, and brushed right away. Then he was turned out into a paddock by the barn. Already, the brown colt was known to have an alpha per-sonality, so another alpha young horse was found to be turned out with him. All that first week, he was either in his stall or turned out with a young gray Thoroughbred named El Kabeir. In the cool of the day, they would run and play.

While he was settling in, all necessary steps were taken to protect his health. His shots were brought up to date, to ensure that he was vaccinated against diseases that could threaten his life and career. All along, he was given pre-ventatives against worms, because picking up parasites in infested soil was always possible. And his teeth—oh, those teeth! By now his permanent teeth were pushing out his baby teeth, and since he was a male, he would eventually have forty, whereas a female horse would have thirty-six.

But unlike the teeth of a human, his would keep grow-ing in length until he was twenty-five or thirty. Back in the day when horses were a main form of transportation, the saying "long in the tooth"—meaning old—was common, since buying a horse took as much care as purchasing a car does today. "Long in the tooth" has trickled down from those days in America's horse culture to be said about lots of things that do not pertain to a horse. As well as that old warning "Don't look a gift horse in the mouth!"

Since the colt's teeth would keep growing, sharp edges would develop and have to be filed down in a procedure called "floating." In those first days when the bay colt was at his new training center, he was visited by the vet and the horse dentist. His "wolf" teeth were pulled. These small extra premolars in front of his back molars could bang against a bit and cause discomfort. And his hooves, which are analogous to humans' fingernails, were also filed and shaped. Then shoes were tacked on.

Thank goodness, all that's over! the colt probably thought, if his thoughts could be translated into English. Now, finally, he was good to go.

Two assistant trainers, experienced in working with the young Thoroughbreds, walked into his stall. One carried a bridle; the other was there to help if needed, as well as to provide safety, similar to a spotter for a gymnast.

Now the real lessons were starting. Schooling for the next seven months would amount to first grade all the way through high school. The young colt pricked his ears and stood showing no signs of anxiety. He viewed the men with that air of aloofness that spoke of his confidence.

One trainer held the bridle up and put a snaffle bit in the young colt's mouth. Of course, he was already used to having a bit from the chifney. But he found that this new snaffle was gentle and forgiving. It was made up of two metal sections that connected in the middle, so it was pliable and rested mostly on the corners of his mouth.

There in the stall, he was taught to bend his neck in response to one rein being pulled, then another. He next learned to turn his body with his head. He walked in circles in the stall, sometimes being aimed at the wall to teach him to turn. Through it all, the trainer used words and sounds. A click or a smooching sound meant to go forward. "Whoa" was said over and over to, well, *Whoa!* Knowing how to stop was all-important for a Thoroughbred. *Whoa* was the golden word.

In a matter of days, an exercise saddle was strapped onto the bay colt. Later, a trainer lay across it. In another day or so, David Smith, an ex-jockey, climbed up into the saddle.

To memorize his lesson in turning, the young colt was ridden toward the wall in the stall. After a couple of days of carrying David Smith in small circles in the stall, the helper stepped out. Throughout all these lessons, the young colt was found to be cooperative and smart. The word *kind* was now used to describe him, which in horsemen's terms means that when a young horse is asked for a certain behavior, he gives it willingly.

Willing, indeed he was. So now Littleprincessemma's colt was taken out of the stall, and with a rider aboard, he walked around the barn in the shedrow eight times. This was a distance of one-eighth of a mile, and soon he was practicing being ridden with other horses coming toward him and behind him, passing him.

Since the shedrow was enclosed with plastic fencing, it was safe. Clearly, Littleprincessemma's colt liked to work. Clearly too, he loved human attention.

Whenever J. B. and his wife, Leigh, went to the barns on Sundays to check over everything, Leigh found Little-princessemma's colt looking over the top of his stall door. As he begged for attention, Leigh petted and scratched him for nearly an hour, and he never seemed to get enough.

Soon he was taken to the practice racetrack on the farm. That was when the real problem surfaced. All the young horses in training were galloped with a buddy. But when the bay colt set off on the track with a buddy beside him, his competitive nature burst out like an uncontrolled fire. He took off, and nothing could slow him down.

For days, J. B. yelled to the colt's rider, "Man, that's too fast! Slow 'im down. Slow 'im down!"

And when the exercise rider called out, "I can't! I can't!" they stopped running the colt with a buddy and let him learn to gallop and control his speed alone.

Soon he was polished in knowing how to answer a rider's signal to slow, to wait, to aim in toward the rail, or out. He knew to switch leads around a turn, changing from his right leg leading his galloping stride to his left, or whichever was needed to help keep his balance. He did it on the fly as smoothly as if warm syrup were being poured on something very delicious—only in this case, it was delicious speed.

When December came, Zayat Stables held an online contest to name its 2014 crop of two-year-old Thoroughbreds. From a small town in Missouri, a nurse sent in the winning name for Littleprincessemma's colt: *American Pharaoh.*

The name made sense: he was the son of Pioneerof the Nile. He had an owner who came to America from Egypt. And *pharaoh* was the title for an ancient Egyptian king.

The winning name was submitted to the Jockey Club in

January to meet the February cutoff date for all two-year-old Thoroughbreds to be registered. The name was sent in as *American Pharoah*. The winner said she'd looked it up before spelling it. Zayat Stables said they submitted it to the Jockey Club with the spelling just as it had been sent in to them. The Jockey Club said they registered the colt exactly as the eighteen-letter requirement was received.

So American Pharoah was *American Pharoah*, misspelled and as American as he could get since there was no time for those who named him to check the letters that would go down on paper. Furthermore, no one was ready to take either blame or credit for the unique name that would one day travel across the globe as one of the world's greatest new sports stars.

The colt didn't care.

◄ HOW THOROUGHBRED RACEHORSES ►
GET THEIR NAMES

By February of its two-year-old year, a Thoroughbred must be named—or a late fee will be charged by the Jockey Club, the governing body that makes rules for horse racing. An owner submits six names in order of preference. The Jockey Club then decides which name the owner can have by how it meets their rules.

There are a lot of rules. Here are some:

- Horses' names can be up to eighteen characters, including spaces and punctuation.
- No well-known initials such as COD, IOU., etc. can be used.
- No names ending in "filly," colt," "stud, "mare," "stallion," or any similar horse-related term.
- No names consisting entirely of numbers. Numbers above thirty may be used if they are spelled out.
- No names ending with a numerical designation, such as "2nd" or "3rd," whether or not such a designation is spelled out.
- No names of actual people can be used unless written permission to use the name is on file with the Jockey Club.
- A name can be changed for a fee, unless the horse has already raced or been bred.

A tattoo under the horse's upper lip is required for all horses that race in North America and is a link between the horse and its registration information. After American Pharoah was named, to avoid confusion for the public and those betting on his races, the correct and incorrectly spelled versions were placed on the list of names that can never be used again. Therefore, there will never be another American Pharoah. There won't be an American *Pharaoh*, either.

12

A BOY NAMED BOB

ONE MORNING IN 1963, fifty-one years before the bay colt was named, Bill Baffert—whose nickname was the Chief—watched his son, Bob, rush out the door of their ranch house in Nogales, Arizona, near the Mexican border, and head to the barn. There, in the early-morning light before school, ten-year-old Bob tended to the quarter horses that his father had bought to go along with the cattle and chickens on the ranch. Then Bob would saddle one of the horses, swing up, gallop to the homemade dirt track in a plowed-over hay field, and let it run.

With hoof-thunder rivaling a summer storm—and an adrenaline rush rising unlike any other two minutes that he could live—he rode the unequaled power of the animal's hindquarters, racing the short distance before the rocketlike explosion was spent.

The Chief often stood watching—his hair graying, his soft brown eyes revealing a mix of love and concern. He was silently hoping that his son Bob would not get himself killed riding the horses at those breakneck speeds. At least, please not before school. And please, not ever.

Bob's mother, Elinora, known as Ellie, mother to the six other kids in the family, would often stop to check on Bob also in her hustle to get off to work as a teacher. She needed to make sure that he would arrive back at the house alive and uninjured in time to get to school. She was a slight woman with a stylish flair. Her parents had immigrated from Spain, and she was fluent in both Spanish and English. Above all, she was a caring mother to her seven children.

Even at the age of ten, Bob was well aware of how the Chief and Ellie worked from sunrise to well into the night, maintaining the cattle ranch and their large family. Always, too, his parents supported his dreams. Early on, everyone in the family knew one sure thing about Bob: his falling off a horse was no deterrent. Getting stepped on did not diminish his passion.

Get up. Get back on. Speed was too sweet not to feel.

As we already know in this story, when the calling is heard, there is not much a human can do but answer. Young Bob Baffert heard it and knew that his love for horses would drive him for the rest of his life.

Triple Crown champion Secretariat, with jockey Ron Turcotte, after victory at the Preakness Stakes, in 1973.

American Pharoah as a foal.

American Pharoah having a treat in stall number 28 at the Churchill Downs stables.

Bath time for American Pharoah after workout at Churchill Downs, Kentucky.

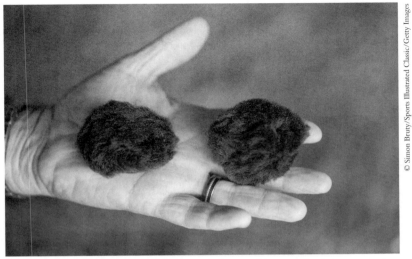

American Pharoah's earplugs ensure he isn't distracted by sounds of the racetrack.

American Pharoah's groomer, Eduardo Luna, prepares him for a morning ride at Churchill Downs. In the foreground is American Pharoah's saddle.

Groomer Eduardo Luna tapes American Pharoah's leg before a workout at Churchill Downs, Kentucky.

Jockey Victor Espinoza and American Pharoah, victors at the Kentucky Derby, as they blast by Gary Stevens on Firing Line. First leg of the Triple Crown, May 2, 2015.

Victor Espinoza and American Pharoah in the Churchill Downs winner's circle after their Kentucky Derby victory.

American Pharoah and jockey Victor Espinoza win the Preakness Stakes at Pimlico Race Course, May 16, 2015.

Victor Espinoza and American Pharoah, the first horse to win racing's Triple Crown in thirty-seven years, win the Belmont Stakes at Belmont Race Track, June 6, 2015.

Jockey Victor Espinoza, owner Ahmed Zayat, trainer Bob Baffert, and their families celebrate the Triple Crown victory.

American Pharoah at Bob Baffert's barn at Santa Anita Park in California.

Trophies for the Kentucky Derby and Triple Crown displayed at Churchill Downs, Kentucky.

Exercise jockey Georgie Alvarez prepares American Pharoah for the Breeders' Cup Classic, which he won, making him the first horse to win a historic Grand Slam in horse racing.

His mother noted that Bob always saw the bright side of whatever happened. He had an air of confidence. When he sold eggs for his father, he made deals with buyers, looking for the best way to get the job done. Living out on a ranch, isolated, with no television, he was close to everyone in his family. He learned early how to get along with people—which would surely serve him well. Growing up so near the Mexican border, where so many neighbors spoke only Spanish, he enhanced the Spanish his mother taught him until he spoke the language naturally and well.

But it was horses he cared about most.

As he spent hours with them, he began figuring out horses' emotions. The first time a horse ran away with him, he realized that pulling on the reins to stop it was no more use than chasing an eagle with a hairnet. He sensed that the horse locked up on the bit out of fear. It was as if Bob had a special sense, a way to read what was going on with a horse. He would study the way it stood and the look in its eye. Reading those signs, along with a dozen other subtle signals, he could know—or at least have the best possible guess—what a particular animal was feeling: surprised, angry, sad, afraid, happy, even disgusted.

Bob's father also noted that by the time Bob was twelve,

he had the ability to tell right away if a horse had the "fire" to race. The Chief himself had a few racing quarter horses and wanted to learn more about the sport. He was amazed at his son and later recalled, "You'd look at this skinny kid and would never think he'd ever be able to handle these kinds of horses, but he trained everything—yearlings and two-year-olds—and galloped them."

By the time Bob was fifteen, he'd heard about the quarter-horse racing strip on the outskirts of town. The desire to race a horse against another is as universal as two ancient horsemen meeting on a trail, chatting awhile, eyeing each other, and then issuing a mutual challenge: "I bet my horse is faster than yours."

Bob and his dad hooked up a horse trailer to the Chief's red-and-white truck, then loaded up Bob's stocky bay quarter horse and headed out to the racing strip. After they unloaded the horse, they set about putting together the gear to help Bob stay on because their plan was to race the horse without the weight of a saddle.

That was their strategy—but then horse racing can bring out any number of wacky, or superstitious, ways of doing things. One of the most famous is described in William Faulkner's novel *The Reivers*, in which a horse gets a whiff of a sardine that unleashes in him blistering speed. Holding up a sardine in front of Bob's horse was not the plan this time. No, Bob and his father's scheme for Bob's debut race was more about how to keep Bob on.

Bob put a golf ball in each of his jeans pockets. Then he swung up on his horse, bareback. His dad wrapped an elastic girth around both the horse and Bob. The golf balls in Bob's pockets were supposed to give some resistance, something to stop the strap from slipping down his thighs like a Hula-hoop.

Then, with Bob aboard, the Chief led the horse to the starting gate. The racecourse was just a big field with a strip mowed in it. The Chief got into the gate to make sure Bob was okay. He uttered a few words of encouragement and then, "Be careful."

Up until that moment, Bob had been excited. But now, in the starting gate, the reality of what he was about to do hit him. Nervousness tingled throughout his body, and when the starting gate opened, he nervously popped his crop on his horse's shoulder for a quick getaway. The big bay spooked, taking off like his tail was on fire.

Suddenly Bob realized that he and his horse were galloping right for a barbed-wire fence. He had no control over the big bay at all. Worse, he couldn't jump off because he was strapped on.

Just as Bob was steeling himself for a crash, thinking, *Oh man, I bet this is gonna hurt!* the horse straightened himself and joined the race. They didn't win, but at least they finished in one piece.

Bob turned his horse around and trotted back to his dad. The Chief calmly looked at him and said, "You know, Bob, I don't think strapping you on is a good idea."

Relieved that he'd live to race another day, Bob went home. Then he kept returning. Hanging around at those backcountry tracks with other horsemen who shared a love of speed taught him the value of pedigrees. He learned what good breeding could lead to.

Now he became serious about wanting to be a jockey. He and his dad had an exercise saddle made. When they put it on his father's favorite mare at a track in the tiny town of Sonoita, Arizona, Bob fell off three times. With a few more tries, he got the hang of it and raced that mare that day and many times afterward. The horse was teaching him the game. Day after day, he trained her, sometimes too long. Whenever she "told" him she'd had enough, he learned to listen.

It soon became clear that Bob had a knack for coaxing speed out of a horse. He also had a knack for knowing how to keep horses willing and eager. When problems arose, his father always said, "Don't worry. No matter what the problem is, we can deal with it."

One day his father picked him up from high school and took him to Tubac, Arizona, to ride a Thoroughbred in a match race. The owner paid him fifty dollars, which, as a freshman in high school in the 1960s, seemed a fortune to Bob.

Soon after, he and his father went out and bought him jockey pants and a real racing saddle. He had silks made up. His feet were too big for jockey boots, so a pair was made for him too. Every night, Bob would lock his bedroom door, put on the jockey silks, get in front of the mirror, and pretend that he was riding.

While his mother always supported his passion, she was rattled at the idea of him riding in races. She had watched him run around the house as a little boy, with a flyswatter in his hand as a jockey's whip. But racing real horses was something else. She so feared for his safety that at his races she would get behind a building and listen to the race call without watching.

One day Bob and his dad were training a horse in a

starting gate. They needed someone to pull the lever, and they asked her to do it. She stood at the starting gate. The Chief got behind the horse, ready to slap its hindquarters for a fast start. "One, two, three," he yelled, "pull the lever!" At that moment, Bob himself whooped to the horse for a quick start. His mother thought Bob was screaming because he was falling off, and she started crying. When she realized that Bob was okay, she said in her schoolteacher voice, "Don't you ever scare me like that again!"

Those backcountry tracks taught him the good, the bad, and the ugly that can always worm their way into a sport when money and betting are involved. Later, at real, established racetracks, knowing that a governing board was in place to keep the rules enforced was a comforting revelation. He weathered it all, driven by his love for horses themselves, as well as the thrill of what horses can do.

By the time he graduated from high school, he was riding in three-hundred-yard quarter-horse match races, and often winning. Then he put his racing aside to go off to college.

At the University of Arizona, he earned a bachelor's degree in animal sciences. Afterward, he tried substitute teaching, all the while keeping up a little quarter-horse racing on the side. When he grew too big to be a jockey, he reconciled himself to that fact by concentrating on training.

He also began noticing gray creeping into his hair. When a gray hair appeared, he pulled it out. Then, when the new ones began popping out with the speed of a salt-shaker, he stopped fighting it. By the age of thirty, his hair would be completely white, something he inherited from his grandfather on his mother's side.

At a track in Tucson, after he won a big quarter-horse race as a trainer, horse owners took note. Soon he was training other people's horses and beginning to think that horse training could become a career.

His life as a trainer took on a 24-7 schedule. Every day he looked over each horse, trying to enter its mind. Was something making it happy, or worried? By then he knew: if you love the horse, it will respond. Calmness and focus were connected to the speed button.

One day, a prominent owner, Mike Pegram, a wealthy fast-food businessman, suggested that Bob try training Thoroughbreds. Taking the suggestion, Bob drove to an Arizona Thoroughbred racetrack in his pickup truck. As usual, he was wearing his cowboy boots and hat.

The track seemed like another world. The owners had on Rolex watches and drove fancy cars. Often the horses were temperamental and required great caution and care.

Bob was scared to death but pretended not to be.

While picking the brains of established trainers—especially the famous, successful ones—he gave himself three years to make it as a Thoroughbred trainer. If he didn't succeed, he promised himself he'd leave.

He moved to California, the racehorse hub with so many tracks. He took out a trainer's license at the Los Alamitos Race Course. He married and had four children.

Unlike some trainers, he believed that horses thrive on work. From his time spent with quarter horses, he knew that the power engine from a horse's hindquarters needed to be developed for quick starts. He set vigorous daily schedules to stoke a Thoroughbred's fire for speed.

He also believed that through constant work, a young horse's bones and muscles were made stronger. To keep the horses interested, he varied workouts. But workouts were workouts. And none were skipped unless an injury or illness required time off.

Bob, too, took no days off. Early every morning, he watched his horses run. In the fuzzy dawn light, he talked to exercise riders by walkie-talkie, telling them how far to go and how hard to push. It was a real boon now to be fluent in Spanish. With so many immigrants from Mexico and South America being employed at racetracks, giving his instructions in their language meant mistakes were avoided. Communications with exercise riders, grooms, and barn workers were direct and straight on,

After workouts, back at the stalls that he rented at the Santa Anita racetrack, he checked on each horse's appetite and behavior, looking for those little nuances that sent signals. Was the horse feeling good, sick, bored, eager?

Success began filling his record books. More victories meant more owners knocking on the barn door. More good horses kept coming his way. In 1996 he had a horse, Cavonnier, that qualified for the Derby.

That May, when Bob stood at Churchill Downs, looking at the famous Twin Spires that marked the racetrack, he realized what that moment meant. He had twenty years of training stored up. He had made it to the pinnacle of the sport.

All that week, from up in the famous grandstand, he watched the races that were run before the Derby. There was nothing like that feeling of seeing horses charging out of the gate, of hearing the roar from the crowd, the sight of those splendid animals unleashing their inborn love of speed. He more than loved being there; being there was becoming a part of him that he could not give up.

The day before the Derby, he got nervous, *really* nervous. Cavonnier was a brave horse. But the dark bay was about to meet the best of the best. Bob also knew Cavonnier had a chance to place, if not win.

The day of the Derby, Cavonnier went calmly to the track. The big bay broke cleanly from the gate and was in a great spot going into the first turn. Bob breathlessly watched Cavonnier rating six lengths off the pace behind the leaders. Then, at the three-eighths pole, Cavonnier's expert jockey, Chris McCarron, moved the horse to the middle of the track. Bob knew now it was just a matter of whether Cavonnier was good enough.

Suddenly Cavonnier started flying: fourth, third, second. Cavonnier took over the lead. "I can't believe this," Bob kept saying. "I can't believe this!"

For so many years, he had dreamed of having a Derby winner. When it really started to happen, he was overwhelmed with feeling.

Near the finish line, Grindstone, a swift, tough horse, slipped up to cross the wire for a photo finish. For agonizing minutes, Bob and the Kentucky Derby crowd waited in suspense while track officials studied the photograph. A moment later, Grindstone's name flashed on the board as the winner. Cavonnier was declared second.

Bob Baffert had taken a horse to his first Kentucky Derby. He had not won, but he knew what it *felt* like to win the Kentucky Derby—*really* knew. Being at the famous race with a horse that he had trained—had spent each day with, had hoped and dreamed for its promise to be fulfilled—was an indescribable feeling. He had to get back; he simply *had to get back*. . . .

⧏ THE DIFFERENCE BETWEEN QUARTER HORSE ⧐ AND THOROUGHBRED RACING

Spanish horses in colonial America were bred with English horses that were brought to America in the 1700s. The native horse and the English horse resulted in a compact muscular animal used for plowing and cattle work. This crossbred horse migrated west with the pioneers, where it achieved fame as the horse of the cowboys.

Its compact frame with massive hindquarters gave it the ability to leap straight into a gallop from a standing start. Over the short distance of a quarter of a mile it was seen to be faster than other horses; hence its name: quarter horse.

As a sprinter, the quarter horse adapted over generations to produce different amounts of muscle fibers. Muscles are simply bundles of stringy fibers that are attached to bones by tendons. These bundles have different types of fibers within them. The quarter horse developed more Type II B muscle fibers, which allow it to accelerate rapidly.

Type II B fibers are fast-twitch fibers, allowing muscles to contract quickly for a great deal of power and speed. Type I fibers are slow-twitch fibers, which allow muscles to work for longer periods of time for greater endurance. Type II A fibers are in the middle; they allow the muscles to generate both speed and endurance. Thoroughbreds possess more Type II A muscle fibers than quarter horses or Arabians; thus, they can propel themselves forward at great speed and maintain it for an extended distance.

When the idea came to race quarter horses, laying a full mile of track was so expensive that a straight track of four hundred meters, or a quarter of a mile, was substituted. That became the standard racing distance.

Quarter-horse races are run flat out at top speed, which means there is less jockeying for position; and many races end with several horses grouped together at the finish line. The track surface is similar to that of Thoroughbred racing, usually dirt.

The training of quarter horses is designed to condition them for quick starts in electrifying bursts of speed. Sprinting exercises are appropriate but have to be moderate to fit a young horse's skeleton and mental immaturity.

The first quarter-mile-length race was held in Henrico County, Virginia, in 1664, which makes horse racing the oldest sport in America. There was no track; there was only a race of two horses running down the village streets. The following year, the first track for Thoroughbreds was laid on Long Island, New York.

Today there are more than seventy Thoroughbred racetracks in the United States and some forty tracks for quarter-horse racing. The excitement of racing has never diminished, for man or horse.

13

THE CHARM AND THE APPETITE

THE DESIRE TO get back to the Derby was now a daily longing for Bob Baffert. In 1996 he saw the video of a two-year-old gray Thoroughbred at an Ocala, Florida, sale. Brothers and horsemen Kevin and J. B. McKathan had seen the horse and sent the video.

The horse's name was Silver Charm. With no dazzling pedigree to catch the eye of a buyer, there was nothing to predict that this gray two-year-old colt would be a great racehorse. That is, not to someone who was not Bob Baffert. With his feel for what added up to speed in a young horse, Bob could read from the look in the colt's eye, its build, and the mechanics of its movement the rare ability that few others could see. Even in watching only a video of the colt running, he instantly knew that this horse had the right stuff.

Bob recommended the colt to well-known Thorough-bred owners Bob and Beverly Lewis. After they bought him, the gray two-year-old was sent to California to Bob Baffert to train.

Soon after Silver Charm arrived at Baffert's barn at the Santa Anita track in Los Angeles County, Bob put the colt to work. He learned that the gray colt was smokin' fast. He was also smart and laid-back, which made him look lazy. Actually, he loved competition and would run only as fast as necessary to keep another horse from passing him. In most ways, Silver Charm was like a big pet.

Sometimes the gray colt would even go to the track for a workout with his head down and his bottom lip hanging, as if he were having a catnap. Yet once on the rack, it was a different story. Silver Charm had abnormal grit and a burning fever for speed.

After training him up to being fit and ready, Bob decided to unleash Silver Charm in a six-furlong race. It was a day on which the extraordinary horse Cigar would be running in a later race. Cigar was trying to break the famous Citation's record of sixteen straight wins. So there were a lot of people at the Santa Anita track that day.

Bob wanted to show off Silver Charm. He was also

hoping that this would be the horse to get him back to the Derby.

Silver Charm lost—which raised doubts in Bob's mind that he might have misread the colt's talent and bravery. Still, he thought the colt was worth a second chance.

He was right. By the time Silver Charm was three, he had won enough races to qualify for the Derby.

That May of 1997, in Louisville, Kentucky, at the famous Churchill Downs track, Silver Charm was so cool and calm going through the tunnel to the starting gate that Bob thought, *Uh-oh*. He feared the young horse wouldn't be awake enough to unleash his blistering speed.

In the last few minutes heading to the track, Silver Charm coiled and flexed his muscles. Bob read the sign and breathed a sigh of relief. Silver Charm had "his game on." He was ready.

With Gary Stevens as jockey, Silver Charm flew down the racetrack, hanging on to his slight lead in the home-stretch. Bob knew that whenever Silver Charm heard horses coming up to try to take the lead, he got mad and steamed up. The colt could pull out his stubborn streak and dig in, which was what he did in the 1997 stretch run in that Derby.

He won by a head.

He also won the Preakness.

He was headed to the Belmont with a chance at the Triple Crown.

There, in the last leg of the elusive Triple Crown, Silver Charm was beaten by three-quarters of a length by Touch Gold, who snuck up on him and passed, just before the finish line.

By then, the Charm and Bob Baffert were bonded in special ways. Silver Charm had done more than take Bob back to the Derby. He had given him a taste of going for the Triple Crown. That became an appetizer for what Bob sensed could be attained.

That next year, 1998, Bob made the decision to run Silver Charm in the Dubai World Cup in the Middle East, the richest race in the world. Along with the desire to win, Bob wanted the Charm to be remembered as more than a horse who'd merely touched noses with the Triple Crown. He wanted the colt to be known as a great racehorse worthy of the Hall of Fame.

Silver Charm was put on an airplane and flown over ahead of Bob. When Bob himself got there, he found the Charm in a plush air-conditioned stall. The horse was living the high life and loving it.

On the day of the race, Bob led Silver Charm over to the track. *Uh-oh,* Bob thought. *What's going on?* The now four-year-old stallion had his head down; his bottom lip was hanging; he looked more interested in napping than running. Worried, Bob rubbed ice water over the Charm's head, hoping to perk him up.

In the saddling paddock, Bob told Gary Stevens, "He's a little quiet."

"That's okay," Stevens said. "We want him quiet."

When Bob saw the Charm go off with the lead pony, he read the signs: the Charm's muscles were coiling. By the time the gray four-year-old got to the starting gate, he was on his toes, pumped up, and sharp.

In the race itself, the Charm lay just off the pace behind a few others. When he pulled in front and headed down the long stretch for home, other horses came charging. Bob yelled, "Oh, no, they're going to run by him!" But then, just as he knew the Charm could do, the horse's stubborn side kicked in. He opened up more speed. It was an awesome thing to watch. Silver Charm won by a nose.

To Bob, it was a great feeling to see the Charm put on a show like that for everyone half a world away. He loved seeing people appreciate the magnificence of the gray colt.

As the trainer who thought so much of the horse, he was proud to be a part of Silver Charm's achievement. But even more, he had come to love the Charm with unwavering devotion and admiration.

Back in the States, Bob went with Silver Charm to Churchill Downs for a secret prank. It was a day soon after the Derby. He dressed Silver Charm up in Arab garb that he'd gotten in Dubai. He himself dressed in a dishdasha, the familiar white Arabian garment, which he'd also gotten in Dubai. He then led Silver Charm onto the track at Churchill Downs and got up on his back with the famous Twin Spires in the background. There, the two posed for the fans to see.

Silver Charm wasn't thrilled about that "dressing up." But by then the horse and his trainer were two good friends doing favors for each other. Together, they had gone for the Triple Crown. Together, they had won the Dubai Cup. Together, they had made Silver Charm known as more than a horse who had come within a length of the Triple Crown. Bob now knew what a taste of the Triple Crown was like. He had been close enough to almost reach out and touch the thrill of it. He had a healthy appetite to satisfy his hunger with a win.

He was famous; he was respected; he was a target for

criticism. His stable swelled to sometimes even one hundred horses in training. He supervised up to forty employees.

In the late 1990s, Bob had two more stars that almost gave him the Triple Crown: Real Quiet and War Emblem. Real Quiet lost in the Belmont by the heartbreaking length of a nose. Poor War Emblem, jinxed with his stumble out of the gate, was beaten by nineteen lengths.

All the while, Bob's parents called after every big race. The Chief and Ellie watched Bob on TV. They stayed close in Bob's life, as they did with all the kids in the family. The strength and support they offered never waned. In the race-horse business, that emotional support was golden. It was the sustenance that fed the staying power.

Riding the ups and downs was a daily challenge for him, just as for jockeys, owners, and all others connected with the sport. The loss of a race, or a sick horse, could wreck a good mood. Learning to ride the highs and lows required an inner serenity that was hard to acquire. Horses, too, can pout when they sense they have lost to a more aggressive competitor. Mood changes were part of the game.

In 2001 Bob got divorced, and the next year he remarried. He and his second wife, Jill, had a son, Bode. In 2012 he was again in Dubai for the World Cup race with a horse named Game On Dude. It was one month after Littleprincessemma's colt was born in Kentucky. There in Dubai one evening, Jill began to suspect that Bob's sudden attack of indigestion was not indigestion. She researched his symptoms on the Internet and found out that his pain described a heart attack.

An ambulance rushed him to a hospital. "I thought I was toast," he said, waking up from surgery that inserted stents to relieve blockages in his heart.

Arriving back home in the United States, he was met by one of the darkest times in his life. His dear mother, Ellie, had died in June of 2011. And now his father, the Chief, distraught from losing Ellie, began to weaken. The Chief's health was failing.

Bob, recuperating from his own heart surgery, found that his recent close call with death was giving him a new perspective on life—how fleeting, how fragile it can be. Now he faced the loss of the father who was so dear to him.

Along with that new crisis was the constant pressure of being a public personality. Potshots, criticism, the hunt for missteps, anything to fuel rumors to distort perceptions of him as a trainer—those never ceased.

His father died in his sleep on September 3, 2012. Gone

now was the anchor in his life, the witty Chief, leaving the memory of love and support that could never be equaled. Trailing too was the memory of the Chief's voice saying, "No matter what the problem is, we can deal with it."

Now the problem was dealing with the sorrow. Days were sucked dry with grief. Training horses left no time for real mourning. There seemed no promise of relief.

By the spring of 2014, the famous trainer was worn down—a more patient man but desperately in need of some good news. That March he sat in his main barn at Santa Anita Park, looking over the list of the new two-year-olds that would soon be arriving for him to train. The name of one caught his eye.

He batted flies—the constant companion in a barn with so many horses—and looked again at the name: American Pharoah. Was that the way to spell *Pharoah*? He didn't think so; but then, there was no time to look it up.

In two months, the young horse would arrive.

Soon the bay colt with the floating walk and kind temperament—now also wearing a funny name—would come speed-roaring into Bob's life.

14

"JUMPIN' JEHOSHAPHAT, HE'S A FREAK!"

AN OLD SAYING expresses both surprise and awe through two words, which are often said when no other words will do. *Jumpin'* and *Jehoshaphat*—saying them quickly together gets the job done.

Early on the morning of March 23, 2014, at the McKathan Brothers Farm in Florida, those two words would best convey what the humans felt as they watched at the training racetrack when the two-year-old American Pharoah was breezed.

In *breezing* he would be allowed to go at a fast speed—maybe about thirty to forty miles an hour—for a certain distance. The rider would give no encouragement—that is, there would be no use of a jockey's whip or urging through the reins. Breezing is simply a way to time a horse's fast workout to see if he is ready to race and train.

For two-year-old racehorses, a breezing workout is a precursor of what might be their future success. In two months, American Pharoah would be sent to Bob Baffert's training stable in California to begin his racing career. His breezing times would be on his record, much like an incoming student's test scores.

On that extraordinary day, American Pharoah was tacked up in saddle and bridle. He had grown to 16.1 hands. With four inches to each hand, he stood five feet five inches at the top of his shoulder. His long neck placed his head well above that. Certainly, he was no weakling. Even being racehorse lean, he was so well-muscled that he weighed over half a ton.

Fog was lifting in the early light. Ahmed Zayat and his son, Justin, had come from New Jersey to see the Pioneerof the Nile colt, as well as the other two-year-olds they had in training there. A small group of people joined them in the viewing stand. Their laughter and joking joined the sounds of neighing horses, the clanging of feed buckets, and the usual early-morning birdsong.

A gray horse, also saddled, stood waiting to lead the bay colt to the practice track. With the chatter coming from the viewing stand, few noticed the young woman, Susan Montanye, the breeze rider, swinging up on the bay colt now named American Pharoah. She was to breeze him one fourth of a mile. The average time for a quarter breeze is about twenty-four seconds.

Susan specialized in showing young horses in these workouts. She'd been told that the bay colt was aggressive, that he was hard to slow down. Knowing this, she was prepared to protect him, to keep him from hurting himself by too much enthusiasm. By now, another rider had mounted the gray lead pony, and together the two horses headed to the track.

For some time, American Pharoah simply trotted beside his lead-pony buddy. Then the pony faded off to the side, and the bay colt, at Susan's cue, lifted into a rhythmical canter with its three-beat gait like a gentle rocking horse. His short tail trailed behind like a feather duster.

Susan rode him on contact, with the racing snaffle acting as the instant messenger holding him to a slow speed. His head was perpendicular to the ground with his nose tucked in. His neck was arched, while his legs beneath him seemed to move like a separate machine in a slow gallop. But then, when Susan got to the pole marking distance, she quickly, as if striking a match, eased her wrists and fingers and crouched close to the colt's back.

Instantly, American Pharoah recognized the signal. As if exhaling and uttering, *Well, thank goodness! It sure took you humans long enough!* he dug into the track dirt with his powerful rear engine and blasted forward like a rocket ignited. His short tail now looked like a flag wildly bouncing in the wind.

In the way that a hunting dog takes after a rabbit, or a hawk swoops down on its prey, the bay colt sped forward with a ferocious joy. He seemed to fly over the track's surface in a smooth-as-silk motion that Susan could barely feel.

The efficiency of his stride left no wasted motion, no misuse of energy. There was no drum-major flashiness, just a breathtaking display of speed for the sake of speed. No stopwatch in his intentions. No scores, no expectations, no human needs, trophies, or dollar-bill dreams. He was simply being who he was and unleashing his unique physical gifts. In doing so, he was revealing who he was in the only language he knew.

The crowd stopped talking. The morning was suddenly frozen in silence. All eyes were turned to see what was almost impossible to believe. Then someone yelled out, "Jumpin' Jehoshaphat, he's a freak!"

As Susan Montanye stood higher in her stirrups, the colt checked himself back to a gallop, then a canter, then eventually down to a trot. Susan let him take his time coming out of that short display of blistering speed. He had the fastest breeze of any of the two-year-olds showing off their talent that day. Eventually, he was walking back toward the barn.

So it was known that he was good. It was just not known *how* good.

Much like the colored glass in a kaleidoscope, his inborn abilities and training would fall together into a breathtaking design. Soon now, soon . . .

However, *that* was not what was twirling in the colt's mind. He was focused on the usual practice at the training farm: the fat flake of alfalfa hay that waited in each horse's stall after a workout. To a horse, that was like a huge fudge brownie with a dollop of ice cream.

Following a walk to cool him out, he was turned loose in his stall. There, he quickly dug into the alfalfa with a possessive vigor that warned: *Don't you dare touch this!*

15

CALIFORNIA, HERE I COME!

THE VAN THAT delivered American Pharoah to Bob Baffert's training stable stopped first in Los Alamitos at the trainer's second barn. There the young horse stayed for a few weeks—which was no problem for Pharoah. Being in new places felt routine to him.

Soon he was loaded up again and taken to Bob Baffert's barn at the Santa Anita racetrack in Los Angeles County. When he was led off the horse van, the first thing Bob noticed was that stringy tail. Wow! For a cool dude of a horse with stellar breezing times, it was like looking at an NFL quarterback with toilet paper on his shoe.

He called for Eduardo Luna, also known as Lalo, who had been employed as a groom for several years. Lalo, with his kind face and graying hair, spoke little English and displayed a quiet, sure way around a temperamental Thoroughbred. As an immigrant from Colima, a state in Mexico, he had a horseman's knowledge from growing up in a rodeo culture.

Always, Bob had been impressed with Lalo's diligent care of any horse assigned to him. So recently he'd promised Lalo a special horse to care for. And now here it was—this tall bay with a chewed-off tail and a misspelled name. Lalo didn't care. Fancy names and tails were of no more importance to him than a weather report: here today and gone tomorrow. Besides, to a groom, a pitiful tail is a happy challenge.

As Pharoah settled into the training-barn routine—a jog or gallop for a mile in the morning, followed by a cooldown in the walking ring, a bath, then breakfast of sweet feed and cooked oats—his extraordinary temperament was discovered and held in awe. Soon Bob Baffert would say, "Every day is a good day with him." He noted that Pharoah lay down several times throughout the day to rest, which he considered a sign of a smart horse. Then, when Bob saw him gallop, he realized that he'd never seen a horse move like that—so natural, so effortless, so like music. He also noted that Pharoah had an air about him that was impossible to describe. It was something akin to an inner knowledge, a secret confidence, as if the young horse knew exactly what he was meant to achieve. But then, a good racehorse has to have more than promise. No one could predict grit. Grit could be revealed only by a challenge. When the young horse was pressed, would he shake off a voice pleading, *Give up, give up, give up?*

Soon, when Lalo came into the barn at five a.m. in the fuzzy light, Pharoah began nickering to him. Lalo would speak back a cheerful greeting in Spanish. Then he would unwrap Pharoah's standing bandages, that had given support and protected his legs from nicks and scrapes, and tack him up for his morning exercise.

The training barn's routine was like a clock keeping time. Through it all, Lalo spoke soothing Spanish to Pharoah and kept his water buckets filled and his hay rack full of sweet-smelling hay. Soon Lalo could recognize every one of Pharoah's whinnies and nickers and what they each meant.

While the afternoons were kept quiet, free of visitors and activities so that all the horses could rest, Lalo waited. Then, at three, he brushed and groomed Pharoah and served his evening meal. At seven p.m. the barn lights were turned off.

When Lalo learned that Pharoah didn't like the mint treats that were a common reward in Baffert's stable, he held out one of the baby carrots that Jill Baffert brought to the barn. Jill had grown up in the polite southern culture of Tennessee. As one of those rare people who could join up with the passion of someone she loved, she supported Bob's devotion to horses and racing as the centerpiece in her life. Trained as a journalist, blond, and eye-catching, she watched over her husband, their son Bode, and Bob's loyal staff. She was a frequent visitor to the Santa Anita stable. When she offered Pharoah a carrot, his lips wriggled over her palm to gently pick it up. Then he chomped it with a cracking sound. And sniffed for more.

Soon he was trying to pick the pockets of everyone carrying a carrot when they stopped by to pet him. So Lalo kept a ready supply of the organic baby carrots in the barn refrigerator.

Lalo began to say in the little bit of English he knew, "This horse's name is American Pharoah, but he speaks Spanish." By then, too, it was clear: Lalo was "Pharoah's human."

As summer drew near, it was time to get Pharoah ready for his first race. Bob Baffert's plan was to enter the colt in a Del Mar Racetrack's "maiden" race, meaning the race was for a horse who had not yet won a race. It would be short—six and a half furlongs, equal to thirteen-sixteenths of a mile or 1,308 meters. His next race would then be decided.

Bob Baffert was thinking that second race might well be the Grade I Del Mar Futurity for seven furlongs, or seven-eighths of a mile. It was a race that was highly regarded; it carried good prize money and would be a good path to the Derby. After all, this was a horse that both owner and trainer were hoping would be their Derby horse.

Exercise rider Jorge Alvarez galloped Pharoah to build muscle and stamina. Martin Garcia rode Pharoah for breezing and more serious workouts. Martin would also be his jockey in his first race.

Martin Garcia had immigrated to the United States from Veracruz, Mexico, and after working for a while in a delicatessen, honed his riding skills and became a jockey. He was compact, muscular, and kind. He had a knack for estimating a racehorse's pace and effort. Beyond being a top jockey, he truly loved animals. He had a feel for them; he could read a horse's mind as well as anyone. He was a true horseman.

Whenever it was to be a breezing workout, Martin Garcia followed Bob Baffert's usual technique: clipping a walkie-talkie to his chest while Baffert held the other part. During Pharoah's workout, trainer and jockey could then talk about how the young horse was doing and plan the workout accordingly.

Every time the bay colt was worked, Bob Baffert saw a different dimension to him. His running action derived mostly from his conformation, the way he was built. The sharp angle of his shoulder allowed him to reach farther with his front legs in his stride. He had an uncanny effortless manner of pulling his hind legs beneath him before bounding forward, somewhat like a rabbit. His stride, which was estimated to be about twenty-six feet, was efficient and powerful at the same time. American Pharoah had all the physical attributes of a great racehorse: speed, stamina, and soundness. But while outwardly he had all the right stuff— big muscular hindquarters, a strong back, a deep chest, and well-formed knees with lots of bone—it was his "heart" that had not yet been tested. His heart, his desire to win, was what no one could see.

Journalists began watching Pharoah as a promising prospect for the big races. Baffert talked about the colt this way: "We've had a lot of good horses. I've never had one that moves like this. Never."

Privately, he always added the hope that the biology gods would keep the young horse healthy.

As Martin Garcia breezed the colt, he noted that for a young horse, "a baby really," Pharoah seemed to just get better and better. In Garcia's experience, he saw so many young horses get tired. But not Pharoah. The colt loved running more than even organic baby carrots. Well, maybe . . .

In any case, it was now August, time for the brown two-year-old with the misspelled name and chewed-off tail to run his first race.

16

GLORY ... OR BUST?

LEADING PHAROAH TO the starting gate would, of course, have to be the lead pony, Smokey. By then, American Pharoah was known to have a special affinity for the little six-year-old buckskin, inches shorter than Pharoah. Smokey claimed a successful career as a reining horse under his official name This Whiz Shines. The little tan horse could stop on a dime, slide like an Olympic skier, and spin like a top in competition. But none of that was needed here.

As a lead pony, Smokey's disposition was his claim to fame. He was definitely a cool dude. Known as "bomb-proof," he could be counted on to let overhead planes roar, bulldozers drive up behind him, crowds scream and flap papers—and he'd do nothing. Not even the opening of an umbrella, which was the undoing of many horses, could unhinge him. His calmness was contagious to a young Thoroughbred, who counted on other horses to signal if there was anything around to be feared.

Nine other horses were entered in this Del Mar maiden race for six and a half furlongs, a short race of thirteen-sixteenths of a mile. With Pharoah's pedigree reflecting distance runners on his sire's side and speed on his dam's side, this first race would call mostly on his speed genes. On race day, August 9, everything was carried out as if this were a day like any other. Schedule and routine were comforting to a young racehorse.

Lalo fed and groomed him as always. He was walked and bathed and handled just as if this day was ordinary. But what Pharoah couldn't see were the crowds of people coming to the racetrack, finding seats, or standing at the rail. In the late afternoon at race time, Lalo led Pharoah to the racetrack. Martin Garcia, as his jockey, was given a leg up. Even though Pharoah had been schooled many times here, in the saddling paddock and starting gate, it had always been in the mornings. Few horses or people had been here. Now there was a crowd, and the noise that came with it. Not even Smokey could make the young Pharoah feel calm. Something was happening that he didn't understand.

He went . . . well, pretty much bonkers—tossing his head, turning in circles, skittering around like a leaf picked up by a puff of wind.

It was as if he remembered nothing: not how to go

into a starting gate, not how to stand, not how to listen to his speed song, nothing. . . . The noise and the contagious excitement from the other immature two-year-olds had set his nerves on edge.

To make it all worse, a human had put blinkers on him. While those cuplike things next to their eyes might be comforting to other horses—making them look straight ahead and focus—he preferred seeing who might be sneaking up on him. As he waited for the starting bell, he was sweating like a thief with snitched goods in his pocket.

He also wore a shadow roll—a fuzzy fabric covering his bridle's noseband—which Bob Baffert customarily used on all his horses. Not only did it prevent a downward glance at a shadow that might spook a young Thoroughbred, but also, and more important, it stopped track dirt from being thrown up in his eyes. That was no problem; it was the noise and the blinkers that were unhinging him.

His usual breezing jockey, Martin Garcia, was at a loss—out of tricks to refocus the young horse. Before now, they had never been together in a situation like this.

Then, *bam!* That harsh bell went off, the gates banged opened, and Pharoah nearly jumped out of his skin.

As he ran with those nine others, he wondered where they

were going. Was something chasing them? Was this herd heading to safety? Did the guy in the lead know? What? Where? Oh—they were all over, beside him, behind him! Everybody was running like there was a fire licking their heels.

Then, before he could figure all this out, it was over.

He reached the finish line in a perplexing fifth place. This race certainly had not been glory. This had been a bust.

Puzzled, Bob Baffert walked slowly back to the barn, studying the colt. Only too well did he know that horses were not machines. They could always come up with unpredictable behaviors. Now he used his imagination to jump that distance between horse and man. He needed to get inside American Pharoah's mind to try to figure out what had been bothering him.

In time, he came up with decisions to try another jockey, to take the blinkers off, and to do something about the noise. After all, Pharoah had not heard a racehorse crowd before. Bob realized that he should have schooled the young horse better—taken him to the track at race time and let him just stand there and watch and hear a race.

Each horse was different. Each one had to be figured out.

If indeed the colt had been undone by all the unexpected

whiz, bang, buzz, snorts, yells, and human chatter, then stuffing cotton in his ears might help next time. It was worth a try.

Despite the shocking loss of the colt's first race, no one lost faith in him. Instead Bob Baffert and Ahmed Zayat went ahead with their plan to run him a month later in the Grade I Del Mar Futurity. That race would have him in the company of the best two-year-olds on the West Coast.

Every day Lalo continued to speak encouragement to Pharoah. As he brushed him, combing his mane and his short tail, he spoke to him in sweet-sounding Spanish. The carrot treats continued to come too.

Now Bob Baffert sent word to Victor Espinoza. Years before, in 2002, he and Victor had teamed up for War Emblem's chance at the Triple Crown. But of course War Emblem's stumble out of the gate in the Belmont had nixed that chance. However, through it all, Bob Baffert had been impressed with Victor's reputation for being consistently calm as a jockey. That calmness might be just what Pharoah needed now. Besides, a new rider could make Pharoah think that this time would be different.

So Bob Baffert sent word to Victor: Would he like to ride this new two-year-old American Pharoah?

Victor sent back, "Okay, I'll ride him for you, Bob."

The Grade I Del Mar Futurity was just under a mile. Eight other tough horses were entered.

In the saddling paddock, Bob said to Victor, "Whatever you do, just send him. Just send him to the front."

Victor took note of the colt's color. While bays are predominant in the Thoroughbred breed, it's unusual to see one with no chrome anywhere: *chrome* being the horseman's term for "white." Victor was intrigued that Pharoah was consistently brown everywhere except for the black on his legs, the black of his mane and tail, and that slight swirl of white on his forehead. Right away, too, Victor noticed that ridiculously short tail. When he asked Jimmy Barnes, Bob Baffert's assistant, about it, Barnes replied that no one knew why the tail was that way, but it didn't affect the colt's speed. Certainly, the tail was of no concern to Pharoah. To him, it was only a problem in swishing away flies.

Then Jimmy Barnes gave Victor a leg up. Jimmy then led Pharoah with Victor aboard out of the saddling paddock toward the tunnel to the track. As he did, he looked up at Victor in the saddle and explained, "I'm going to take you, because he's a little crazy. The first time he ran was a nightmare."

Victor felt a sudden jolt of concern. *Oh boy,* he thought. *Now I know why they put me on!*

This time, though, with cotton in his ears, no blinkers, and with Smokey warming him up, Pharoah was calm, cool, and collected. The cotton in his ears allowed in only muted sound, enough to hear the starting bell, but not the hysterical sound of a crowd cheering or screaming encouragement to their favorites.

As soon as the bell sounded and the starting gates flew open, Pharoah blasted off to take the lead. In only a few strides, he got into his high cruising speed. *Wow!* Victor thought. *It feels different. It feels like there's so much power there. He's like a swimmer gliding through water.*

Pharoah, with Victor in the saddle, went flying across the finish line with that short tail bobbing like a snare drummer's solo in a rock song. They won by four and a half lengths, with no one coming close enough to catch them.

Now Bob Baffert knew he had the horse he expected.

Lalo proudly led Pharoah into the winner's circle. Then he led him back to the stable, where he carefully wrapped the horse's legs in standing bandages. Of course, too, he gave Pharoah enough carrots for him to know that he'd certainly done something very, very right.

Ahmed Zayat stayed in New Jersey during these first two races. He had horses running at other tracks. Bob Baffert filled him in by phone. But now, with the colt's first commanding win, they both knew they had a horse worthy of the Derby.

In the weeks that followed, Pharoah turned in breezing workouts of four furlongs in forty-eight seconds as if he were just strolling to Starbucks for an early-morning coffee.

In figuring out the young two-year-old, Bob Baffert and his assistant Jimmy Barnes, along with exercise rider Jorge Alvarez, breeze rider Martin Garcia, and Lalo and Victor were becoming a team.

Now they were ready for Pharoah's third race.

The Grade I FrontRunner Stakes on September 27, 2014, was conveniently at the Santa Anita track for eight and a half furlongs, exactly one and one-sixteenth of a mile in a field of ten.

This time, the race was like the same song, second verse. Pharoah and Victor blasted out of the starting gate and went streaming across the finish line by three and one-quarter lengths.

Pharoah was now seen as a contender for the most prestigious race for two-year-olds: the Breeders' Cup Juvenile.

That celebrated yearly race showed off new talent. A win in that race would make Pharoah the most highly acclaimed two-year-old. The race was held at different tracks each year, but this year it would be held again at the Santa Anita track, where Pharoah was already stabled.

Convenient indeed.

His workout times—along with his two impressive wins in respected races—put him at the top of the list to be considered for the Eclipse Award as the top two-year-old Thoroughbred.

Impressive indeed.

A week before the Breeders' Cup Juvenile, Martin Garcia took Pharoah out for a breeze of five-eighths of a mile. The colt ran it in one minute flat, a sizzling workout. Even more impressive, the young horse looked like a kid who'd just been let out on a playground. All the while, Pharoah ran with his ears pricked forward as if licking his lips with joy. Even more impressive—when he came back to the barn, he was barely blowing.

He was so strong.

Then, on Monday, October 27, only five days before the Breeders' Cup Juvenile, Lalo was walking the colt in the shedrow when Bob Baffert noticed a slight give as the colt put weight on his left front leg. Right away, he called a veterinarian.

Nothing wrong could be found. Bob coached himself to stay cool, even though he was distressed. He called Ahmed Zayat in New Jersey. "It's not soft tissue; it's not bone," he said. Then he assured the owner that the vets were doing everything they could to diagnose the mysterious lameness. However, the Breeders' Cup Juvenile might be out.

Zayat was crushed. He agreed with Bob's wisdom, though. He said, "This horse was going to run away with that race. But when he's that special and that good, you treat him as such."

Bob was devastated too. He'd never had a colt like this, and now to see Pharoah lame—it was a tough pill to swallow. Indeed, "It's sickening," he said to anyone listening. All he could do was to stop the workouts and find the cause.

Over the next few days, no vet could find a definite answer. Every day Bob Baffert dreaded going to the barn. Seeing Pharoah laid up was too much, too much emotional pain. And no way to relieve it.

He had to do something, though, anything—surely he could do something. . . . On the off chance that Pharoah might have a deep bruise in that hoof, Baffert decided to soak the foot in hopes of relieving the soreness. Lalo lovingly soaked the hoof in warm water, then rewrapped Pharoah's legs in standing bandages. After a few days, the young horse seemed somewhat better. He was sound at the walk, even though at a jog, the slight lameness was still detectable.

Now it was necessary to announce Pharoah's withdrawal from the Breeders' Cup Juvenile. In a press conference, Bob announced that American Pharoah was being scratched from the important race and added, "The timing is a killer. We all know how valuable a horse he is. I don't want to risk it."

Owner Ahmed Zayat flew to Santa Anita to see the horse and meet the journalists. He put it this way: "Everyone was gushing over him. A lot goes wrong. It takes a lot of perseverance. You have to have the personality for it. The vets can't find anything wrong with him. But you have to do right by the horse, so they do right by you. It's too much risk to run him now."

So Pharoah was taken out of training.

Each day going to the barn, Bob Baffert felt physically sick, thinking his star might be forever lost to some undetected injury. All the while, the veterinarians working on

Pharoah were figuring it out. Finally, the colt was diagnosed with a high suspensory strain, which was like a human's soreness from overextending a knee.

Rest was the prescription.

After a few weeks of complete rest, Lalo began walking Pharoah slowly in the mornings. The rest of the day, Pharoah watched all those humans bustle around in the barn doing chores. Every morning at dawn, a lot of other horses were going to the track to work. Since Bob Baffert had so many horses in training and so many employees, there was a lot of activity. With the majority of the workers native Spanish speakers, the sounds Pharoah heard were familiar and soothing.

If it was fun to lay off, to stand around, watching everyone else run, Pharoah didn't say. But his horse language sometimes made it clear that he would prefer to be "out there," as he looked longingly at the track. He delighted at seeing "his human," Lalo, who waited on his every need. He took comfort in the closeness of his loyal sidekick, Smokey.

His stall was next to Jimmy Barnes's office. Everyone kept an eye on the young horse as they passed by.

Being hand-walked around the barn in the shedrow kept him somewhat fit and relieved of boredom. Otherwise, he hung his head over his stall guard and watched with his soft, gentle eyes. His friendly expression enticed those passing by to come rub his forehead, to speak to him with their human, soothing sounds. Always, he begged for a carrot. Occasionally a smell would reach him from somewhere in the barn, and his lips would curl up as if he were laughing. His response was only a flehmen reflex, set off when his sensitive membranes were stimulated by something with a strong odor. But humans found delight in his gesture and spoke to him and laughed in return.

All in all, it was clear: he'd prefer running to being benched.

On January 1, 2015, he officially turned three. Finally, after two months, the troublesome lameness healed. Jorge Alvarez took him out for short jogs. He appeared sound and ready. Thirteen days later he was awarded the title of the top two-year-old despite missing the Breeders' Cup Juvenile. His accomplishments so far were too impressive for the racing world to forget.

Soon, he was galloping his usual one and a half miles. Then Martin Garcia began breezing him. The colt responded with glee. He was fit, fast, and ready. He also now read the signals: when Jorge Alvarez climbed aboard, Pharoah knew he would gallop at a steady pace, and he was obedient and calm. He could be so calm with Jorge in the saddle that Jorge could park him on the track with his feet out of the stirrups while they watched the others go by.

But when Martin Garcia walked into the barn, Pharoah knew it would be "go" time. He got eager and aggressive. He could hardly wait to rev up the wings on his feet.

Bob Baffert and Martin Garcia were always careful, monitoring his every move. Through their walkie-talkies they discussed how the colt felt. As the distances of his workouts lengthened, the sounds through their walkie-talkies became whispers. Their reverence for the strength of the colt took on hushed tones, as if they were gazing at a masterpiece in a museum.

Baffert and everyone else at the barn were ecstatic. He was back! Pharoah was back! He was not going to have to retire from a promising racing career after all. Hallelujah and start the party!

Pharoah and his team once again began climbing the slippery slope of racing glory.

In March, it had been five months since his injury. It was now time to put him back on a racing schedule, one that would aim him for the Kentucky Derby. First off was to be the Grade I Rebel Stakes at Oaklawn Park in Hot Springs, Arkansas.

Eight days before the race, Martin Garcia breezed Pharoah in a final workout. All went well, but as Garcia rode Pharoah back to the barn, he could feel that Pharoah was uncomfortable on his left front foot. With a horseman's sensitive feel, Garcia could also tell that Pharoah's knee was not the sore spot; it was his hoof.

A bruise seemed to be on the underside of that foot. It couldn't be readily seen, but a good horseman's guess was the best guess. And Bob Baffert was an excellent horseman. In the years when he was climbing up the success ladder as a trainer, he'd done his share of wrapping horses' legs, bathing them, rubbing them down, treating all sorts of athletic injuries, even sleeping beside them when they were sick. He now focused on mechanics.

Working with his favorite farrier, Wes Champagne, Baffert agreed to try a new type of shoe on Pharoah. The colt was fitted with a shoe that would protect his left foot more completely. It was a design that the farrier made especially for him: a thick sheet of aluminum alloy was attached over the back part of a regular shoe. The solid plate covered Pharoah's heel and part of his frog, which is the triangular-shaped structure in the underside of the hoof that nature designed to help minimize slipping and promote circulation. The frog is a very important part of a horse's anatomy.

Again, Pharoah was fit, ready, and eager. Like preparing any athlete for competition, his team dealt with the detours from perfection and fixed them. Minute-by-minute care was the norm. They were winning at their job of maintaining a superlative athlete.

Getting to the Rebel Stakes was not simple. Pharoah was put on an equine air transport to fly to the race to be run on the fourteenth of that March. His legs were wrapped in thick standing bandages for protection, and he wore bell boots over his front hooves to prevent his shoes from being torn off should a back foot accidentally step on the edge of a front shoe.

Boarding a plane was different but not scary, not with Smokey leading the way up the long ramp and then standing in a stall right next to him—even if Smokey did try to steal more than his share of the hay hanging between them. On occasion Smokey would put his ears flat on his head in horse language to warn his young friend to *Watch it, bro!* as if saying, *I don't care who you are; it's my job to keep you in line.*

Flying required some pretty smart balancing and the endurance of lots of noise. Only fancy horses ever got to do this. But then, Pharoah never thought of himself as fancy; all he cared about was being with Smokey and getting his share of the "sweet-cake hay." Helpful too was the cotton in his ears that had become a part of his "public wardrobe."

The Grade I Rebel Stakes, as a race of eight and a half furlongs—equal to one and one-sixteenth of a mile— would be good training for a colt whose trainer and owner had great plans for him. It was especially appropriate, too, with his being racing fit. Although the length was the same as the FrontRunner Stakes, this race required travel and running on an unfamiliar track. The Kentucky Derby was ten furlongs, a mile and a fourth. Giving the young horse experience with longer races was smart training.

The goal was to follow that up a month later with the Arkansas Derby—nine furlongs, a mile and one-eighth in a field of eight. These two races should be a good path to the Kentucky Derby, which on the first Saturday in May, would be a promise of lasting glory.

The schedule was the perfect preparation for a colt with so much promise.

How the bay colt would handle all this was the part that no one could answer.

⚑ QUALIFYING FOR THE DERBY: ⚑
THE POINTS AND THE RULES

The purpose of horses qualifying to run in the Kentucky Derby is to make certain that the field of up to twenty horses can compete at the distance of one and one-fourth miles. The race is limited to only Thoroughbreds that are three years old.

In 2013 the officials at Churchill Downs, where the Kentucky Derby is run, started a system to qualify horses ranked on points rather than on how much money a horse has won in races. These points are earned by a horse's performances in what are known as Derby prep races.

Most horses begin racing in their two-year-old year. The top four finishers in Derby prep races earn points determined by their placement: first, second, third, or fourth. Any three-year-old horses that race early after the January 1 of their third birthdays also earn points to qualify for the Derby.

The Kentucky Derby at Churchill Downs in Louisville, Kentucky, is the most famous, a cultural tradition called "the most exciting two minutes in sport." The day before the Derby, fillies race in the Kentucky Oaks, their own race equal to that of the colts running in the Derby. They too are qualified on a point system.

In 2015 nineteen races were held in various parts of the country between September and February to award points to qualify for the Derby. The most points were earned by the first four finishers in the Breeders' Cup Juvenile, which is a race held each fall, usually at different racetracks; the Delta Jackpot in Vinton, Louisiana; and the Champagne Stakes at Belmont Park in Elmont, New York.

Six other well-known Derby preps are the Florida Derby at Gulfstream Park near Miami; the Louisiana Derby at the Fair Grounds in New Orleans; the Wood Memorial at Aqueduct Racetrack in New York; the Santa Anita Derby at Santa Anita Park in Los Angeles County; the Arkansas Derby at Oaklawn Park in Hot Springs, Arkansas; and the Blue Grass Stakes at Keeneland Racecourse in Lexington, Kentucky. The UAE (the United Arab Emirates race) in Dubai also counts.

Eight races held before the prep races also award points: the Risen Star Stakes at the New Orleans Fair Grounds; the Fountain of Youth at Gulfstream Park; the Gotham at Aqueduct in New York; the Tampa Bay Derby at Tampa Bay Downs in Tampa, Florida; the San Felipe at Santa Anita Park in California; the Rebel Stakes at Oaklawn Park in Hot Springs, Arkansas; the Spiral at Turfway, in Florence, Kentucky; and the Sunland Derby at Sunland Park in New Mexico.

In addition, two races run just weeks before the 2015 Derby awarded the four finishers points: the Derby Trial at Churchill Downs and the Lexington Stakes at Keeneland, both in Kentucky.

Most of these are Grade I races, which have a governing board titled the American Graded Stakes Committee of the Thoroughbred Owners and Breeders Association. The "stake" or entry fee is what owners must pay to enter their horse in the race. The racetrack adds an additional amount of prize money to be paid to first-, second-, third-, and usually fourth-place finishers.

The American Graded Stakes Committee has criteria to qualify stakes races. These are:

- The race has a purse of more than $75,000.
- The race has been run for two years under the same conditions.
- The horses are tested for the use of illegal drugs, and that testing is managed by a governmental authority.
- If toe grabs—mechanical additions to the shoes to give more grip on the racetrack surface—are used on the horses' shoes, those toe grabs cannot be longer than two millimeters.

The points that horses win by succeeding in their chosen races are tallied. The top twenty point earners qualify for the Derby. As in any sport, each contestant must adhere to the rules.

17

` 'AS HIS MOTHER A UDDER?

ON THE AFTERNOON of March 14, 2015, at Oaklawn Park in Hot Springs, Arkansas, the bay colt was saddled. Victor, his permanent race jockey now, was given a leg up. Ahmed Zayat had flown in from New Jersey to see his colt run. Bob Baffert was home in California to watch the race on TV. He was cutting down on travel, trying to protect his health after his near-fatal heart attack three years before. His assistant, Jimmy Barnes, had traveled to the Rebel Stakes with Pharoah and, of course, Lalo.

Before the Pharoah team left California, Bob had instructed Victor to take the colt slow. They didn't want to overdo his first time back racing.

With Victor in the saddle, dangling his feet casually, Jimmy Barnes led the horse and jockey toward the track among the seven other horses in the race. Victor hadn't been on the colt during his layoff; only Jorge Alvarez and Martin Garcia had ridden him. Each had said the colt was good to go. Victor could only hope that Pharoah was like he'd been five months before. There was no way to know until he asked the colt for his racing speed.

Suddenly the skies opened and dumped buckets of rain onto the dirt track. It now looked like a piece of used cellophane, shining and gooey, stretching out in the overcast light. The downpour made a little stream near the rail as if it were an official waterway on a map.

Pharoah was expected to run in this? And on his first race back in the game? Was this crazy, or what?

Pharoah had, of course, had workouts in rain—but not in a storm. And not in a race. Ahmed Zayat anxiously called Bob Baffert in California. Should they scratch? Should they take this chance with his return to racing?

Bob said, "No." They couldn't scratch. There was no space in their schedule to make up points for the Derby. Even though this was a Grade II race, there were still points to be earned.

The colt *had* to run in this or miss the Derby.

Did anyone know how Pharoah would likely handle the wet track? Was his mother good at running on a sloppy track? Could you call her a mudder? What about his father? Was *he* a mudder? No one knew for sure. And, it really didn't matter, because Pharoah was Pharoah.

How would he react when mud was thrown up in his face? When his coat was pelted with rain? When his feet landed in puddles splashing up—would he want to stop and go back to the barn? Or would he want to run faster, to find shelter?

What about the earplugs? What would the colt do if they got wet? Should Lalo take them out?

Questions, questions—there were dozens of them and dozens of reasons for one's nerves to get in a tangle. For a moment, the race didn't seem worth taking the chance that Pharoah would be injured. Yet all preparations had been made; everything was set on *Go*.

Victor put his feet in the stirrups. Pharoah was led toward the starting gate.

The earplugs were left in. His shadow roll was in place to block mud slung up, or back at him. (Though, please, don't let it be mud slung *back*, at least for very long!) Victor wore several pairs of goggles, so he could pull down a clean pair when the others were gummed over with mud.

There were six opponents. Pharoah was led into the

starting gate in post position four. A three-year-old named Madefromlucky was the one to watch out for.

The starting bell clanged; the gates flew open. Pharoah stumbled. As he regained his balance, his right front shoe was twisted in the shuffle. Then he hit his stride, unleashing his cruising speed—that sweet, rhythmical motion that Victor thought of as moving like a swimmer through water. On a day like today, how appropriate that comparison was!

When Victor asked, the colt surged forward to take the lead, to be where *he* was the one throwing back mud. And he was giving Madefromlucky a mouthful. He picked up his speed song, *Come and get me. Bet you can't. Bet you can't.*

His ears were pricked. He began singing home in the stretch, lengthening his lead, kicking back mud on Madefromlucky, who now was fading, fading. At the finish line, Pharoah left him behind by six and one-fourth lengths. A sports commentator enthusiastically said, "This was a canter in the park for American Pharoah!"

Back at the barn, Lalo and Jimmy Barnes discovered the twisted shoe. Wow! The colt was held in even more awe. He had run in the rain, ignored a damaged shoe, had run after a long lay-off as well as the stress of being shipped all that distance from California, and still. . . .

He was the one. He was the one they'd hoped for. Maybe even the one everyone hoped for—the one who could coax willingness to believe in something real and good from those who had lost the will to believe in anything real and good. He was keeping his promise. He was as good as expected. As extraordinary as imagined.

Would it last?

Pharoah went back to California to train, then flew back for the Arkansas Derby, April 11. That race should earn him enough points to put him solidly in the Kentucky Derby.

Bob Baffert told Jimmy Barnes that if they won that race he, Lalo, and Pharoah would head straight to Churchill Downs in Louisville from Hot Springs. Again, Bob was staying home in California, cutting down on travel. Besides, he had another Derby horse in training, the impressive Dortmund. He was also hoping that once they got on the Triple Crown trail, he'd be traveling for weeks. Traveling for weeks meant they would be winning.

So, at the same track four weeks later, American Pharoah jogged to the starting gate. This time there were *seven* rivals to outrun. As he was led into his starting post, there were six on his left, and one on his right. Here on the outside, he'd have to run a bit farther, but also from here Victor could size up the race as it took shape. Then he'd use his traffic-dodging skills to guide Pharoah where he needed to be.

Victor also knew that he had to find out something important about Pharoah. He needed to know it before the Derby. If Pharoah couldn't negotiate the Derby's big twenty-horse field, they'd be in trouble. So now, even if it made Bob Baffert angry, Victor was going to try a new tactic with Pharoah. He would ask the colt to *rate*, to slow down and stalk the leaders. Then, when he gave the signal, he'd ask the colt to surge into the lead in the backstretch.

The gates banged open. Victor placed Pharoah four lengths behind the leader and stayed there, stalking like a mountain lion waiting to pounce. Pharoah listened; he relaxed into Victor's soft hands and waited with the obedience of a good partner.

At home in California, Jill and Bob Baffert watched the race on television. When Pharoah seemed to be lagging behind the frontrunners, they were puzzled. In the clubhouse where Ahmed Zayat was watching, he was dumbfounded and worried. He had no idea what Victor was doing. But in California, Bob Baffert suddenly realized that Victor was asking the colt to rate, to use his speed wisely, to use it when called upon. Victor was teaching the colt to finish off his racing skills with the maturity of a professional.

As Victor and Pharoah passed the one-eighth pole, all was fine. Pharoah was just cruising. When they passed the one mile pole, Victor gave the signal. The colt surged forward, seeming to even lower himself onto the track, unleashing an explosion of speed. In California, Bob and Jill Baffert, watching the TV screen, leaned back, smiling, loving Pharoah's spectacular winning performance.

With Pharoah crossing the finish line by eight lengths, the announcer loudly summed it up: "Amerian Pharoah, breakthtaking, in a mesmerizing performance!"

As for Victor, he patted Pharoah and exclaimed, "Man, he's a rocket ship."

◣ FIRST TWO JEWELS IN THE TRIPLE CROWN ◢

Meriwether Lewis Clark Jr., grandson of the famous American explorer, was an enthusiastic horseman. In 1872 he traveled to England to see that country's famous horse race called the Derby. He was so impressed and excited by seeing all the splendid horses, as well as being part of an elegant social event, that he went to Paris to see the greatest race in France, the Grand Prix de Paris at Longchamp. After experiencing these races in Europe, he wanted America to have a similar traditional race.

When Clark returned to America, to his hometown

in Louisville, Kentucky, he organized the Louisville Jockey Club to raise money to build a top-notch racing facility outside the city. The track became known as Churchill Downs, named for John and Henry Churchill, who gave the land for the racetrack.

At first the race was modeled after the English Derby at a distance of one and a half miles, but its length was shortened to a mile and a quarter in 1896. The first race was run by fifteen three-year-old horses on May 17, 1875, in front of a crowd of ten thousand people. A colt named Aristides won, ridden by Oliver Lewis, an African American. Later that year, Jockey Lewis rode Aristides to a second-place finish in the Belmont.

In that first Derby, thirteen of the fifteen jockeys were African American. The trainer Ansel Williamson was a former slave. In fact, African Americans made enormous contributions to horse racing. Before the Civil War, slaves cared for and trained horses, eventually riding them in races. In the 1820s, when horse racing was the most popular sport in America, the largest number of the best trainers and jockeys were African Americans.

Another African American jockey, Isaac Burns Murphy, won the Kentucky Derby three times—in 1884, 1890, and 1891. His record was not broken until 1948, when jockey Eddie Arcaro won his fourth Derby. The last African American to win the Derby as a jockey was James Winkfield in 1901 and 1902.

In the early twentieth century, racial discrimination curtailed African Americans' roles in American horse racing as jockeys and trainers. However, they stayed in the sport as exercise riders, groomers, stable hands, and clockers. Today, in the twenty-first century, these roles are changing. Latino jockeys are frequent winners, and some African Americans are owners.

A few women jockeys have ridden in the Kentucky Derby. The first was Diane Crump, who finished fifteenth in 1970. The sixth female jockey to ride in the Derby was Rosie Napravnik, who finished fifth in 2013, and last in 2014. She also won the Kentucky Oaks, the race for fillies held the day before the Derby, twice—two years in a row.

A few traditions are practiced at the Derby. Women wear big hats. The winning colt is draped in roses, which gives the race the nickname of "the Run for the Roses." The winning filly of the Oaks is draped in lilies. And always the song "My Old Kentucky Home" is sung.

The next jewel in the Triple Crown, the Preakness Stakes at Pimlico Race Course in Baltimore, Maryland, was first run in 1873, two years before the first Kentucky Derby. At one mile and three-sixteenths, it is shorter than the Derby. Pimlico Race Course is the second oldest racetrack, Saratoga being the oldest.

The Preakness winner is draped in a blanket of black-eyed Susans, giving the race the nickname "The Run for the Black-eyed Susans."

The race was named by a former Maryland governor after a winning colt. Eleven times, the Preakness was run before the Derby, and twice on the same day. In 1931 it was set on the third Saturday in May. By that year, the Preakness Stakes was drawing such a large crowd and generating so much racehorse excitement that it was declared the second race for the Triple Crown.

18

EVERYTHING'S COMING UP ROSES

BACK AT BOB BAFFERT'S barn in California, the days may have seemed the same, but they were far different. They now had a Derby horse. Pharoah's points added up to 160, fourth behind the three-year-old named International Star with 171, the unbeaten giant Dortmund with 170, and a keen colt, Carpe Diem, with 164. Pharoah's total earnings from the four races he had run so far were $2,171,026. Right behind him with 113 points was a gray colt, appropriately named Frosted.

The year 2015 had some of the best three-year-olds that the sport of racing had seen. Bob Baffert knew that the next weeks would call on all he had learned over the years in how to train a racehorse. Getting an equine athlete to peak at the right time was an art. No set-in-stone recipe would do. Every day he would have to listen and sense what was best for the horse.

At the Santa Anita stable, Lalo carried out his duties as usual, but the pressure was different. The horse was so valuable now—not that each and every one of them wasn't. But the challenge was to make sure Pharoah did not become sick or injured.

A video camera was placed in his stall. Barn workers could now check on him every minute, and so could Bob Baffert on his iPhone. Any sign of colic or the horse getting cast and thrashing against the wall could hopefully be detected in time to avert a crisis.

Heading to the Kentucky Derby, the question being asked was: How would American Pharoah handle a fight? The Derby was the only race in which twenty horses were allowed to be entered. With twenty bunching together at breakneck speed like a herd fiercely running toward what they could not see or understand, it would be a bar fight to a finish line.

Victor knew that he was going with a special horse to compete in the Derby. Twice before he had won it, so his experience would be a plus. But in the Kentucky Derby, anything could happen, especially in that kind of traffic.

Bob Baffert was also training Dortmund, the big

chestnut that had not yet lost a race. Always, the two colts had been kept apart, stabled at opposite ends of the barn and going to the track for workouts at different times. But now, in the Derby, the two colts would run against each other for the first time.

Dortmund was huge, seventeen hands, which added up to being five feet eight inches at the withers, the top of the shoulder where the mane begins. Dortmund looked like a giraffe, a bullet-fast red giraffe. Martin Garcia was his jockey. But more than Dortmund's fame as being monster big was his love for a fight. He liked to eyeball another alpha colt and dare him to pass.

Dortmund was coming into the Derby undefeated in six races. Martin Garcia liked to say that whenever he raced Dortmund, he didn't really ride him, he was a passenger— because the huge colt just dragged him around. Martin Garcia may have peppered his comments with hyperbole, but clearly Dortmund's strength was daunting. The chestnut was also the son of the former Triple Crown contender Big Brown, which brought Dortmund even more regard.

Now they all flew to Churchill Downs to settle in before the Derby.

In his week of workouts there, Pharoah turned in sizzling

times. One morning, with Martin Garcia onboard, Pharoah ran five-eighths of a mile in :58.40. A less-than-a-minute time caught a lot of attention. There were thirty-two other horses turning in workouts that morning. The Derby had many races all week, so lots of horses were training early each day on the track. Pharoah's workout was the fastest of any. Baffert and Garcia were used to that, but the dazzling workout stirred interest.

Gary Young was one who was dazzled. He had made a career of timing horses' workouts for owners and others who liked to bet on races. He said of Pharoah, "I have been doing this for thirty-five years, and he might be the best horse I've ever seen. He's simply like Michael Jordan and stays in the air like he did in his rookie year. He stays in the air longer than any horse, and you get the feeling that there's not one gear left, but he may have two, three, or four gears."

After that workout, as Pharoah returned to his Churchill Downs stable, Bob Baffert felt goose bumps. Pharoah was not even breathing hard. "From here on out," Bob said, "we have to keep him happy."

The middle of that week was the most hair-raising time for Victor and Bob Baffert. Wednesday was the day for post positions to be drawn. Owners, trainers, jockeys, and journalists crowded together on the second floor of the grandstand.

Nervous anticipation charged the air. Everyone knew that starting gate positions could mean everything. Twenty horses coming out of the starting gate made for a stampede to the first turn. Some described it as being like a "cavalry charge." Horses in the one and two post positions were often squeezed in at the rail and rarely made it to a good running position.

Bob and Victor stood together, listening to the draw. If Pharoah drew the number one or two post, the race could be over before it even started.

The anxiety made Victor nauseous. For a man known to be cucumber-cool, he was now a hash of nerves.

Bob stood by, barely breathing, often holding his breath.

Finally, Pharoah's name was drawn. "Post eighteen." The news was not great, but it *was* a relief. This outside post meant Pharoah would have to run farther than the others in posts closer to the rail. Only one horse had won the Kentucky Derby from post eighteen, and that had been in 1982. But at least Pharoah wouldn't get pinched in near the rail or bogged down in traffic.

Bob Baffert said, "I'm just glad it's over." Then, "I need a hot dog."

All that week, Ahmed Zayat walked excitedly among the stalls, talking to the press. He had two other horses entered: Mr. Z and El Kabeir, the gray colt that had been Pharoah's paddock buddy at the McKathan Brothers training farm.

Zayat took a moment away from the nerve-rattling anticipation to drive his family to the nearby WinStar Farm. Here his horses Paynter, Bodemeister, and Pharoah's father, the second-place Derby finisher Pioneerof the Nile, stood as stallions. When Pioneerof the Nile was led out of his stall, Zayat whispered, "Your son is going to do it for you."

Breaking away from Churchill Downs for a moment too, Bob Baffert drove Jill and Bode an hour away to Georgetown, Kentucky, to a farm for retired racehorses, appropriately named Old Friends.

For a decade Silver Charm had been a breeding stallion in Japan. Recently, though, the Derby and Preakness winner had been moved to Old Friends. Bob had always followed where the horse was, and now, at twenty-one years old, Silver Charm was officially retired. Bob wanted his family to meet the horse that had played such a monumental role in his life.

When Bob, Jill, and ten-year-old Bode walked up to

the pasture fence, Silver Charm was grazing at the top of his paddock. The horse was now white with age. The Charm looked up and saw them. For a moment, the horse seemed to contemplate what humans standing at the fence might mean. Then he came running, tossing his mane, his head held high, his white tail like a kite in the wind of his gallop. The carrots that Bob, Jill, and Bode offered may have had more to do with the horse's eager greeting than his memory of the trainer. But then again, Bob and the Charm had spent a lot of time together.

After all, trainers know that horses' keen memories are what make them trainable. Put good things in a horse's memory, and the lessons stick for good. Put bad things in, and overcoming the habits are harder than unsticking glue. Horses' behaviors always tell their histories. Silver Charm's history was now revealing his trust for the trainer who had always respected his happiness.

"He was such a noble horse," Bob said, emotionally rubbing Silver Charm's head. Bob then thanked the horse for all he had done for him. His love for the horse was evident.

Jill quietly watched, aware of the privilege of sharing this moment. Seeing Bob honor his partnership with the horse that had brought fame and success to both man and horse was making a lasting memory for her, too.

On the morning of May 2, 2015, the 141st running of the Derby, the sun rose high and clear. The day promised to be sun-splashed and mild.

The night before, El Kabeir had been scratched with a swelling in his ankle. Then, on Derby morning, International Star was scratched too.

The field was smaller now, but not by much.

By the middle of the morning, the first of the crowd of 170,000 was trickling in.

Ten other races were being run that day. So by the afternoon, the crowd was loud, excited, and primed for the famous one.

Before a big race, Bob Baffert always practiced two rituals. If he saw a black cat, he immediately turned around and went the other way. That week he made a few tire-squealing U-turns. He also never allowed a hat to be put on a bed. No reason, just *no hats on the bed*. Superstitions of athletes and trainers are always their own private bargains with fate.

Now it was a matter of waiting for the walk-over to the saddling paddock.

Women's elegant hats flapped and nodded in the breeze. The air was electric with anticipation. The National Anthem was sung. Then the song "My Old Kentucky Home," with the whole crowd of thousands joining in, swaying, sometimes tearing up with the sense of the tradition of it all.

In the walk-over, as Lalo led him, Pharoah caught the sense of the crowd, of people running to catch up or to get in front of him. Cameras snapped beside him and over him. He'd never been in a bunch of so many—people in front, people behind him, horses, too, even people hanging over the rail from the infield of the track. All those horses were being led to somewhere. . . . Where? What? It was unnerving for a human but even more for a horse.

His other races had not had this excitement in the air. This was bigger, louder. This was . . . well, enough to set his nerves on edge.

He began fighting Lalo, pulling on the lead. Tossing his head, he jigged. Sweat on his coat turned to lather.

Even though Bob had switched the cotton in his ears for the more solid earplugs that show horses sometimes wore, the noise was getting through. Sensing Pharoah's distress, Bob told Lalo and Jorge Alvarez to get Pharoah out of the middle of the track. Get him out of the procession of horses and put as much distance as possible between Pharoah and the chaos.

When they did, Pharoah relaxed a little. But Bob Baffert had another remedy for his colt's case of nerves. He told Lalo and Jorge to hose down Pharoah in the paddock to cool him off. So they did—taking him a distance away where, somewhat privately, they could turn on the hose and redirect Pharoah's mind. He always loved a bath, and now a soapless shower reminded him of what was routine and fun. He collected himself and began to really relax.

Those who'd been part of his early life came to escort him to be saddled. Just as a family gathered to support one of their own, there was Frances Relihan, who'd weaned him; Dr. VanMeter, the vet who'd been there when he was born; the Taylor Made Farm managers who'd trained him as a yearling; and the McKathan brothers, who'd graduated him from their racehorse high school.

His buddy Smokey was somewhere near, borrowed by the TV interviewer to be ridden up to the winner after the race. In high-pressure times, there is nothing like having a friend close by.

Pharoah was now calm. He'd gotten hold of his nerves—even though he was clearly revved up by reading all the signs that soon he would be allowed to run.

With his outside post, he would be the last to go in. So he and Victor had to wait for the others to be loaded. Victor kept Pharoah calm by riding him in loose, slow circles a distance away from the others. The jockey had on his usual race-time cool. He had the knack of staring nervousness down as if he had ice water coursing in his veins. Sometimes he even chewed gum and blew a bubble while sitting astride a revved-up Thoroughbred. But today there was no gum. No nerves out of control, either.

Nearly half the field was loaded. In post position eight was Pharoah's daunting stablemate, Dortmund.

Most of the eighteen colts had not run against one another. Materiality, waiting in post three, was clearly eager. This would be Pharoah's first meeting with the son of the famed Afleet Alex, who had clipped heels with another horse in the homestretch of the 2005 Preakness, gone almost to his knees, and still won. Afleet Alex was also now famous for being part of Alex Scott's Lemonade Stand to raise funds for cancer research. Diagnosed with cancer herself, Alex Scott, at the age of four, set up a lemonade stand in her front yard to raise money for a cure. Four years later after Alex died, the owners of

Afleet Alex called her parents and asked if they could set up lemonade stands at racetracks to continue Alex's mission. After all, Afleet Alex shared part of her name and was also courageous. As a newborn foal, he'd had a hard start in life—having to be bottle fed—yet had become a champion, winning not only the Preakness but also the Belmont. So no doubt loads of fans would be cheering for Materiality, especially coming into this race undefeated and expected to set the pace.

Now the gray horse, Frosted, was led into post fifteen. He had won the Wood Memorial—a race that often predicts the Derby winner—and was expected to run the leader down. Mubtaahij had come all the way from Dubai in the Middle East as the winner of four races on dirt. A keen colt named Firing Line was waiting in his perfect position, right in the middle of the track, post position ten. He had famed jockey Gary Stevens onboard. The two of them paired up were a force. They were certainly not wimps. It was clear, too, that Stevens had his game face on.

Here, lining up, were the most talented three-year-old Thoroughbreds in decades. No matter when as two-year-olds they had won their first race, they were primed and ready to be here, having proved it in their prep races.

Now it was Pharoah's turn. He was led into post eighteen. Quickly the gate was shut behind him. As usual, he shifted his feet: right, left, back. But there was not long to wait now.

In only a second, the starting bell clanged and the gates banged open. Dortmund jumped out in the lead, followed by Firing Line. After fighting his way from his outside post, Pharoah calmly cruised along in their shadow.

At the half-mile post, the three in the lead were clipping off the distance as if they were metronomes keeping one another's rhythm. When they turned for home, Dortmund cut the corner first; and Firing Line moved to the middle of the track. Victor guided Pharoah to the wide route, far from trouble.

For thirty yards, Gary Stevens had Firing Line matching Dortmund's strides one for one. Then he punched Firing Line's booster power and sped on by.

Pharoah now was no longer cruising but calling on a higher gear. He was confused by the competitive jousting. In his far-out position, he was losing his focus. He wasn't paying attention to the urgent messages that Victor was sending. He didn't realize he was in a neck-and-neck fight. With his Ferdinand-the-bull disposition, he was puzzled.

Dortmund and Firing Line were going at each other with all their natural instincts unleashed: two eager stallions furiously fighting to take over the lead of this herd. Victor needed to get Pharoah to feel the *fight*.

As the rest of the field struggled to keep up, Victor moved Pharoah closer to Firing Line. He crossed his reins and began fanning Pharoah with his whip. Pharoah had never met this kind of test, and Victor knew he would have to ride him hard to win.

Pharoah refocused. *So, okay, this is what a real fight is.* Their weapon was speed, and it was time now to use it. With only a sixteenth of a mile to the wire, Firing Line's booster shot faded. Dortmund was done. Victor's insistent messages woke Pharoah up; he hit the finish mark only a length ahead.

Oh, yes, he had grit. There were no more questions about that. Grit was in his mind, his heart, his muscles. Grit was his backbone, and he'd found it for sure now.

The Kentucky Derby was his. The garland of roses would soon be laid across his withers.

Pulling Pharoah up, Victor exclaimed, "I feel like the luckiest Mexican on earth!"

The television cameras swung around to catch the

Baffert family in the grandstand. Ten-year-old Bode Baffert jumped up and down, waving his arms in an explosive expression of glee. His unfiltered display of deep emotion made adults envious. Many wished that they, too, could jump and yell in childlike abandon.

In their box seats, Ahmed Zayat and his family grabbed one another in exhilarated hugs. After coming so close before, they now had a winner. Justin Zayat became so excited that he threw up, which the cameras caught. Later, embarrassed, he brushed away the moment by making fun of himself. His reaction, though, was proof that winning the Derby, after so many years of trying, meant an enormous amount to the Zayat Stables.

In the winner's circle, Zayat said, "I felt today I came with a star. I was very cautious of saying that because I wanted the horse to do the talking. It is not about what we feel. It is about the horse."

A website headline shouted, "Bob Baffert's 10-Year-Old Son Went Absolutely Nuts Watching American Pharoah Win."

As for Pharoah himself, he had just come out of the hardest fight of his life. He would always remember its lessons.

19

SLOP, O GLORIOUS SLOP!

ONLY TWO WEEKS separated that win from the next leg of the Triple Crown, the Preakness in Baltimore, Maryland. Pharoah stayed at Churchill Downs to train. A few days before May 16, he was sent with Smokey to the Pimlico Race Course in Baltimore.

Here was the grueling schedule of doing all this again in such a short time. The race was shorter by a sixteenth of a mile. Fewer horses would run. But all the same, the race meant traveling, another big crowd, and enormous expectations.

In his workouts, Pharoah showed that he was as strong as ever, even getting stronger. Most young Thoroughbreds drop weight from the schedule of racing and traveling. But Pharoah showed no signs of stress.

Routine was his anchor. Every day the colt was fed, groomed, and worked just as any other day.

On race day he was calm, not unhinged like he had

been by the crowd in Louisville. Jimmy Barnes and Lalo led him to the saddling paddock. Raindrops began to fall as Victor settled into the saddle.

Then a downpour started. Thunder, lightning—it was a storm the likes of which the colt had never faced, not even in the Rebel Stakes two months before.

Golly, this is an insane amount of rain, Victor thought as sheets of rain pelted him and the colt when they were loaded into the starting gate. The fact that Pharoah had run in that sloppy Arkansas race, and won, *did* give Victor some comfort. The colt seemed sure-footed even on a slippery, glasslike track.

Still, this was an unbelievable amount of water being dumped all at once on them. Rain ran into their eyes, dripping down Victor's helmet, sneaking into Pharoah's ears. Oh, those ears—may the earplugs forever stay dry and in place!

This time Pharoah was in post position one. But since there were only seven other colts in the race, getting hemmed in from post one was not such a danger. Besides, Victor and Bob's strategy was to jump out front and stay there. Leading for nine and a half furlongs should not be a problem. Pharoah had already proven he had stamina enough for that, as well as for more.

Calmly Pharoah stood in his post position, waiting for the others to load. He didn't seem perturbed at all. It was as if he were saying, *Raining? Did you say it was raining?*

Again, he faced some of his biggest opponents—the giant Dortmund, the feisty Firing Line, and five others. Dortmund was in post two, just beside him. Next to him was Mr. Z, then Danzig Moon, Tale of Verve, Bodhisattva, and Divining Rod. Firing Line was in the last position, post eight. Divining Rod was bound to be a crowd favorite. He was owned by Roy and Gretchen Jackson, who'd also owned Barbaro, the gallant winner of the 2006 Derby who had broken his leg in the Preakness. The whole nation had been aroused to compassionately follow Barbaro's fight to heal from his injury for eight months, before he lost his life to laminitis, the hoof disease that is a horse's nightmare.

But here now in the rain in the starting gate at the Preakness was not a time to think of injuries or loss. Victor and Pharoah were on their own Triple Crown journey. As usual, Pharoah shifted his feet in the starting gate.

When the bell sounded, and the gates flew open, Pharoah bounded out to take the lead. He stayed there. But then, that was always the best place to avoid mud in the face. Again, it was if he sang all the way to the finish line, *Bet you can't catch me, catch me.*

By seven lengths he sailed across the finish line in front of the others. He was now set up for history. One more win, and the Triple Crown would be his.

The view, though, was chilling. Thirteen other horses, over three decades, had been here before—perched on the edge of history, hoping for a win.

They had all failed.

The reality was, so many three-year-olds were worn out by the third and longest race. After all, that was what the Triple Crown challenged: the ability to last, to meet the grueling test of three big races in a set amount of time: The Derby at a mile and a fourth. Two weeks later, the Preakness, a mile and a sixteenth. Three weeks later, the Belmont in New York, a mile and a half. To win all three required more than normal grit. It required super grit. Only very special horses could pull off a win in the longest race after two others that were no walks in the park. To handle it, one had to have breeding for distance delivered by that mysterious mix of genes.

The Belmont was the nemesis for some, the unwinnable test. The racecourse was nicknamed the Big Sandy.

To Pharoah, it was just another race.

To him, little pleasures mattered too. In most ways, a flake of alfalfa, his buddy Smokey, and a bucket of sweet feed, along with dozens of baby carrots, spelled the height of happiness.

20

INTO THE PAGES OF HISTORY

AFTER THE PREAKNESS, Pharoah returned to Churchill Downs in Kentucky to train for the Belmont. Everyone was eager to see what the recent big races had taken out of him. Each day, his every move and mood were studied.

The reports coming in were not just good news; they were phenomenal. Every day Jorge Alvarez galloped him for fitness and monitored Pharoah's condition. As he dismounted back at the barn, he said, "It didn't seem like he was tired or anything."

Assistant trainer Jimmy Barnes reported, "He's perfect—just the way he always is—so we'll gallop a little bit further [on Saturday], and then by Sunday we'll be back to his normal gallop at a mile and a half."

Martin Garcia, who breezed him, sent a crackling message to Bob Baffert through the walkie-talkie clipped to his chest: "Awesome! Super awesome!" Often he used a Spanish word for "awesome."

Baffert laughed. "*Awesome* is good. *Awesome* is really good."

Awesome became their byword for preparing for the Belmont. By that time too Bob Baffert had come up with a fun, made-up story to answer questions about Pharoah's short tail. He said, "The legend goes that he was running wild in a field, and a mountain lion was chasing him, and that's as close as he could get to him. But nobody really knows."

Two timed workouts were planned—and then, on to New York and the Belmont. Bob realized he was set to accomplish what he had longed for and worked so hard for. But also by now, he had so much admiration for Pharoah's remarkable physical gifts that he wanted the horse to win for his own recognition, to be listed among the greats.

Belmont day, June 6, 2015, was sunny and clear. A blue sky. A kind sun. The racetrack began filling up. The year before, so many people had come to the famous race that, afterward, the wait for a train back to the city had bottled up race fans for hours. This year, planning to avoid that, racetrack officials had limited ticket sales to ninety thousand.

Cell phones buzzed; iPhones flashed. As the crowd found their seats, they stopped to chat. Many knew that while seeing a Triple Crown winner *was* a possibility, expectations should be tempered. After all, in more than three decades no horse had accomplished it. Coming here to have a grand party was a good enough reason to witness the 147th running of the Belmont.

Even Bob Baffert was prepared for a loss—or at least he was warning himself not to get his hopes up. He'd been here three times before with a horse ready to break the dry spell of no Triple Crown winner. He'd always come home empty-handed. So it was wise to keep his hopes in check.

Some in the racing industry were even thinking that the Triple Crown was no longer possible. The statistics were daunting. Over the years, fifty-two horses had won one of the races toward the Triple Crown but had failed to secure all three for the title. Thirteen had earned the right to stand in the starting gate with two wins—the Derby and Preakness—qualifying them to add the Belmont as the last jewel in the crown. And yet . . . and yet . . .

In fact, some people were thinking that to have a modern Thoroughbred win all three races in a harried five weeks might be out of the question. Thoroughbreds were bred lighter for speed. Modern horses had lost some of the traits inherited from the old-time Thoroughbreds, which were heavier and heartier, preserving racing strength for five weeks. Journalists and sports writers pointed out all the reasons that American Pharoah would not win.

The world had changed; horses had changed; it might be time to change the Triple Crown.

In prerace interviews, Bob Baffert's son Bode was of special interest to the media since his unfiltered exhilaration after the Derby win. The video of that, with his exuberant jumping and shouting, was watched by thousands, always eliciting smiles. Now when asked about the Belmont, Bode solemnly replied, "It's *really* a long race."

Above all, the hope was that no one and no horse would be injured.

Lalo led Pharoah to the saddling paddock. By now, crowds bothered Pharoah no more than a distant fly. He found he even liked the human attention of being photographed as well as the hundreds of eyes following him. Still, though, he wore his earplugs. Why change a winning combination?

In the saddling paddock, Bob Baffert said to Victor, "He's ready. Put him on the lead and go for it."

So Victor did.

And now they were heading for the first turn. But since Pharoah leaned back a little in the starting gate, his break was a step behind. So Victor sent him forward with an urgency learned in the Derby.

Hustling to the first turn, Pharoah put Victor just where he wanted to be—out front, leading the thundering herd of seven. Now tactics could mean everything.

At the one-eighth pole, the pumping of Pharoah's heart under Victor's left boot signaled, *No problem.* The colt was breathing like a well-fueled steam engine too. Pharoah had plenty of *go* to do anything Victor asked of him.

Crowd noise now faded into the background. Muffled hoof thunder became a cloud encasing them. The race took on the feel of a dream. Pharoah's hooves seemed to barely skim the track. The trick was for Victor to know where everyone was, to maintain his position, to measure out the colt's strength wisely.

As Pharoah settled into his cruising speed, Victor was again reminded of a swimmer skimming over the water. Now they were close to the half-mile pole. Victor could see it, just ahead.

It was a soft pace. Victor was elated, knowing that meant

Pharoah would not tire quickly. At the first turn, Victor felt so happy, he thought it was the happiest he had been in his whole life!

Behind them, the keen colt Materiality was giving chase. *Steady, steady,* Victor said to himself.

As they came near the one-mile pole, guts and breeding, training and heart mattered most. American Pharoah shook off Materiality. Now others were making a run at him.

At the far turn into the homestretch, the colt from Dubai, Mubtaahij, thundered up, reaching, breathing like a train in full throttle, trying to catch Pharoah. As he got within three lengths, his speed song faded. His endurance ran out. The Dubai colt gave up.

Now sneaking up outside of Pharoah was Frosted. The heralded gray colt was announcing a late challenge. Frosted's jockey was urging him on, shaking the reins, asking the colt for every breath and strength within him to steal the lead.

In answer, the gray colt catapulted himself to four, then three, then two and a half lengths behind Pharoah, hoping to plunge by in the last few yards. The finish line was just ahead.

Victor gave Pharoah his head, and Pharoah exploded in answer. It was as if the colt were elastic, stretching out and seeming to lower himself onto the track. Drawing on the unknown depth of his heart and speed, Pharoah clipped off a four-length lead. The crowd began roaring, yelling with unrestrained excitement. Without expecting it, would they now see something so very rare, so exquisitely singular? Would they, too, be part of this history?

Even Frosted's trainer, who certainly wanted to win the race, realized that he was seeing a horse so rare, so magnificent, that in the last eighth of a mile he began cheering for American Pharoah.

The crowd's roar was deafening.

Ahmed Zayat stood up and waved his arms like a conductor before an orchestra, encouraging the crowd to cheer on and on.

Pharoah was oblivious to it all. He sped past the finish line five and a half lengths ahead and kept galloping while Victor stood in his stirrups, waving and saying over and over, "Wow! Oh, wow! He's just an amazing horse!"

Pharoah galloped out, easing his muscles and bones back down from his history-making speed to a canter, a trot, a walk. Smokey trotted up to him with the television commentator Donna Brothers riding him. She was holding out a microphone to Victor. Lalo rushed to clip a lead on his bridle. To Pharoah, it might have seemed strange that all those humans wore such happy and amazed looks on their faces. To him, he had just run as he loved to run. For him, it was as simple as that.

The record books, however, would say otherwise. He had clocked in at the second-fastest Belmont for a Triple Crown winner: two minutes, twenty-six seconds, and sixty-five one-hundredths of another second (2:26:65), a time just above the great Secretariat's untouchable 1973 Belmont run of two minutes and twenty-four seconds.

In stunned elation, many in the crowd just stood, reluctant to leave, wanting to let the moment sink in, to savor this history, and to behold the rare creature who had given it to them. Victor cantered Pharoah the full length of the grandstand, letting people gaze at him and applaud in delirious appreciation.

Lalo, with tears of emotion, led Pharoah into the winner's circle. Jorge Alvarez watched, close by. Martin Garcia looked up at the TV in the jockeys' room and quietly said to himself, "I knew he would." For him, Pharoah's Triple Crown win was no surprise.

Frances Relihan, who had weaned him, stood near the

winner's circle, savoring the moment for the colt that she had picked out as having great promise.

Baffert's assistant, Jimmy Barnes, ran from the grandstand where he'd watched the race with his wife. He then rushed onto the track to be beside Lalo and Pharoah.

In the winner's circle, Ahmed Zayat said emotionally, "We all wanted it. We wanted it for the sport. This horse represents hope. Hope."

Bob Baffert held up the Triple Crown trophy. He may have made a nice pose for the snapping clicks of the cameras. But inside, there was one hole in the satisfaction he had always imagined at this moment. He was wishing he could call the Chief and his mother, Ellie.

For Victor, his life was changed. Forever changed.

In that moment of crossing the finish line, Pharoah had touched Victor's life and sprinkled it with the rare power to make it different. Even beyond the daily schedule of becoming a celebrity, something deeper was altered. No way now could this bay colt not break through the barrier of protection that Victor, as a jockey, had built over the years. Shielding himself from the heartache of having to leave an animal he had grown close to was not possible this time.

American Pharoah, with his exquisite physical gifts, would be forever entwined with Victor's life.

As for Bob Baffert and Ahmed Zayat, along with Lalo, and all the others who'd worked with Pharoah as he trained for this, as well as his fans—their lives were altered too. For one brief, glorious moment, all of America turned and paid attention to a rare being among them. History had been forced open for a new page to be written.

Pharoah changed his own life too.

The day after the Belmont, he was promised to appear at Churchill Downs for adoring crowds to cheer him. He took his plane from Belmont Park in New York to Kentucky. Waiting for him onboard was Smokey. Together, they shared a bundle of hay while Smokey seemed to say, *I don't care if you are the Triple Crown winner, part of this hay is mine!*

When the plane landed, Smokey was taken to a waiting trailer. Pharoah, with his legs still wrapped in traveling bandages, deplaned and was led onto the van too, and tied in a stall opposite Smokey. There was hay. Having something to munch on during the boring ride to the barn was a nice touch. A police escort beside his trailer ushered him to Churchill Downs.

The next day, thirty thousand fans applauded, savoring the sight of him as he appeared on the track between races.

Soon after, when he returned to Bob Baffert's barn at the California Santa Anita track, movie stars came to see him. Fans wrote him e-mails and sent carrots.

Crowds followed him and simply stared in awe. He was pictured in *Vogue* magazine. His image was ironed onto baseball caps and T-shirts. He was no less than a Babe Ruth, or a Muhammad Ali, or a Michael Jordan: those athletes who rode out the ups and downs of their careers to remain in sportsmen's minds as the ultimate to be revered. Even non-sportsmen recognized the feat of American Pharoah, as did Internet followers, who loved to argue about the colt's accomplishments compared to those of the great Secretariat.

Most would want to remember where they were, and what they were doing, when American Pharoah flew into the pages of history.

If there is any moral to this story—which Pharoah himself wrote by his extraordinary accomplishments—it is that we should never be too busy to look over to see what is happening next to us. It might be a spectacular promise waiting to be fulfilled.

CODA

EVEN THOUGH IT'S not all said and done—because there is much more to be lived in Pharoah's story—what if he could talk? What if he could answer our questions, replying in our human words?

What if we could set aside our constant temptation to project our feelings and thoughts onto him? And, instead, we just listened? Took time to listen?

Would we find that he is chuckling—humoring us as we think that anyone can own him?

As much as we try to jump across the divide between animal and human, the leap cannot be made with accuracy. The scientist Charles Darwin, who studied plants' and animals' abilities to survive, found that all living animals—and yes, even we humans—share six emotions. These universal primary responses are fear, anger, disgust, surprise, sadness, and happiness.

Of course, Darwin also was projecting—throwing his

imagination across the space between species. But he did find that animals' behaviors were prompted by those six distinct reactions. They are our bridge.

So, when it *is* all said and done, and this story of Pharoah is old and passed down and written into the history of the year two thousand and fifteen, certain things will always be true. No one owned Pharoah. He was his sole proprietor. If anyone could be listed as his possessor, it would be the wind and the rain, the earth and the sky, his relentless need to run and his majestic frame spurred by muscle and heart.

For a little while, he simply shared himself with us. For those of us who took the time to look, we were gifted with the renewal of a very important belief: that every once in a while, promises are kept. Every once in a while, perfection and miracles *do* come along. Every once in a while, an unexpected guest travels through our lives, reawakening us to the goose bumps of wonder.

EPILOGUE

AFTER AMERICAN PHAROAH'S Triple Crown achievement, he raced a few more times. As Bob Baffert said about Pharoah, "He's happiest when he's on the racetrack." So, two months after his "crowning," he ran in the Haskell Invitational in New Jersey, and put on a sublime show. He led in front from gate to finish, winning by one and a fourth lengths, even as Victor clearly eased him up to save him.

Three weeks later, in the Travers Stakes in Saratoga, New York, his grueling year of racing and traveling more than eighteen thousand miles, winning eight consecutive races, switching time changes between his home base in California and wherever he was racing began taking its toll. Bob Baffert also thought that perhaps during a prerace workout, when an estimated fifteen thousand people came to see him, Pharoah may have thought *that* was the race and overspent his energy. On race day Pharoah came in second by three-fourths of a length. Other Triple Crown winners, Secretariat, Seattle Slew, and Affirmed, raced after their "crowning" and lost. Coming in less than first place did not tarnish their legacy.

Likewise, American Pharoah's brilliance was undisputed, his legacy secure. Then, on October 31, 2015, five months after he won the Triple Crown, he thrilled all of America when he won the Breeders' Cup Classic in Lexington, Kentucky. Breaking from the gate, leading the whole way of one mile and a fourth with his ears pricked, he ran with such joy that more than history was made. He crossed the finish line six and a half lengths ahead of the field of seven other horses, some older and fresher. He set a new track record of two minutes and seven one-hundredths of a second. Hearts were alight with the embrace of a new American super champion.

Winning the Breeders' Cup, which was established in 1984 as a year-end championship, gave American Pharoah the title of Grand Slam winner. The great Secretariat did not even have the chance to attempt it, since the Breeders' Cup was established eleven years after Secretariat's career. A Triple Crown winner winning the Breeders' Cup was an accomplishment no horse had ever attempted.

In the winner's circle, Bob Baffert said, "This was for

Pharoah. We wanted him to go out the champion he is."

Two days later he was driven a few miles from the Breeders' Cup racetrack at Keeneland, in Lexington, Kentucky, to Coolmore's Ashford Stud Farm to begin his new career producing baby Thoroughbreds with a chance of inheriting his extraordinary blend of traits. To show him the ropes in his new home, a former Derby and Belmont champion, Thunder Gulch, at the age of twenty-three, was assigned to be his next-door paddock mate. It would be Thunder Gulch's job to keep American Pharoah calm, not to risk injury by taking every other young stallion's dare to race each other in their paddocks.

Just off the trailer, American Pharoah stopped and looked around. Lalo led him, tearful at having this close relationship now to be interrupted by distance. He led Pharoah to his new digs, which were plush indeed. The next day, another groom walked Pharoah outside, where he stuck his nose in a clump of grass and settled into the daily life of a beloved horse.

He would not be forgotten. He had run himself into immortality. His story would be a never-ending story for his humans, too.

As the year turned to 2016, Bob Baffert was given

awards for his achievement as Pharoah's trainer. When Bob asked his son Bode what should he say in his acceptance speech, Bode confidently answered, "I would just tell them that you're honored to win this award and you never dreamt when you were a little boy you would win this award. And you still have a little life left in you to maybe win some more."

So yes, Bob Baffert continues to train horses. Yes, too, American Pharoah continues to thrill his fans as they visit him at the breeding farm. He still loves baby carrots, still displays the kind temperament of a golden retriever, and loves visits by the Baffert family and Victor.

AUTHOR'S NOTE

WHEN AMERICAN PHAROAH won the Triple Crown on June 6, 2015, a new hero stepped into our hearts and minds. Here was a real running, breathing animal that seemed to be everyone's favorite pet. This book is a faithful depiction of this event as well as an invitation to learn about the universal nature of a horse.

As I wrote the early pages, it became to me a very American story: so many different people from different places came together to help this one young horse deliver his promise.

I have fleshed out facts from information and interviews that have been published in newspapers and magazines and on the Internet for the public to follow this momentous accomplishment of the first Triple Crown win in thirty-seven years. To verify facts and enrich the story, I've had conversations with many of the principal participants (i.e., some humans) to make sure that I have told Pharoah's story with an accuracy of which he might be proud. I have also attempted to get inside the head and heart of American Pharoah himself to help readers fully understand his extraordinary spirit.

As I delved into the research, I also awakened a "curiosity itch"—a need to pull a thread from some subject to follow it to more understanding. So, for those like me, I have layered this story of American Pharoah with facts of biology, psychology, and American history.

To all children—including the one in me—this book is affectionately dedicated in the hope that American Pharoah's cool, confident joy in being who he is will inspire all of us to strive for excellence. And to realize that all horses, both winners and losers, deserve our care and love. I think Pharoah himself might want to say that.

—SHELLEY FRASER MICKLE

FEBRUARY 28, 2016

ACKNOWLEDGMENTS

SPECIAL THANKS TO Bob and Jill Baffert, who kindly joined up with this project and gave it the ingredients worthy of Pharoah's accomplishments. Jill also kindly allowed me to use the phrase that she coined, "Pharoah's human." And of course Bode, who rides the racehorse life with such grace and excitement, embracing the purpose of this book to delight a world of children. To Victor Espinoza, who shared with me the challenges of coming to America and succeeding beyond what he feared to dream. When I asked him if he had a photo of himself as a child to put in this book, he humbly replied, "I don't think there is one"—which is a stark contrast to our photo-crazy world, where practically every American child's birth, footprints, and first smiles are documented by a camera lens. Super thanks to exercise rider and writer Alex Brown, who was the second person to read the manuscript and in his British e-mail voice offered warm encouragement as well as keeping me straight on racehorse facts. To the McKathan Brothers, who spent a morning showing me how Pharoah was trained as a racehorse. To their farm manager, Chris Alexander, who was fearless in making phone calls to those who could give answers. To Susan Montanye, who shared with me her experience of breezing Pharoah as a young two-year-old, knowing only later the goose-bumping realization that she had ridden a legend. To Frances Relihan, who brought to life Pharoah's weaning. To Brian Beach, Victor's kind agent, and his attorney, Paul Schindler. To Ben Sturner, Pharoah's sports agent, who understands the importance of stories, inspired by his role as father to William and Cameron. To Dr. Tom VanMeter, who verified the time of day when Pharoah was born. To John Hall at Taylor Made Farm, who helped me understand Pharoah's experiences as a yearling. To Martin Garcia, who shared with me his experience of riding Pharoah and made me laugh out loud as he gave playful descriptions that reflect a jockey's necessary resilience. To my husband, Parker, who read the first draft and kindly said, "Wow!" (Husbands risk injury if this is not their first reaction.) To my dearest of friends, Marilyn McLean, who carefully read and corrected the manuscript. To Gretchen Jackson, who with her husband Roy, owned

Barbaro and encouraged me to bring to life this story for future horse-racing fans. To Christa Heschke and Karen Nagel of the New York publishing world, who believed that all children should have a chance to read about this once-in-a-lifetime horse. To Doug Horn and John Smithwick, my Keeneland partners-in-fun. To my childhood friends in McCrory, Arkansas, who came to my and Gloria Bronte's January 1 birthday party for all racehorses, even when we dropped the fudge on the kitchen floor and secretly served it anyway. I owe special thanks to Pharoah himself, who couldn't have cared less that his "biography" was being written but looked me in the eye and seemed to instantly say, "Oh, okay." And then, "Got a carrot?"

APPENDIXES

⊰ THE BELMONT STAKES 2015 ⊱

FINISH	POST	HORSE	JOCKEY	TRAINER
1	5	AMERICAN PHAROAH	VICTOR ESPINOZA	BOB BAFFERT
2	6	FROSTED	JOEL ROSARIO	KIARAN MCLAUGHLIN
3	7	KEEN ICE	KENT DESORMEAUX	DALE ROMANS
4	1	MUBTAAHIJ	IRAD ORTIZ JR.	MICHAEL DE KOCK
5	4.	FRAMMENTO	MIKE SMITH	NICK ZITO
6	3	MADEFROMLUCKY	JAVIER CASTELLANO	TODD PLETCHER
7	2	TALE OF VERVE	GARY STEVENS	DALLAS STEWART
8	8	MATERIALITY	JOHN R. VELAZQUEZ	TODD PLETCHER

The Belmont is the third leg of the Triple Crown—the last
and most arduous test for any racehorse since the Belmont

is the longest race at a mile and a half. For a horse who has won both the Derby and the Preakness, the Belmont is doubly challenging to its endurance. Jerry Bailey, Hall of Fame jockey and horse-racing analyst said, "The Triple Crown is designed to wear a horse out." American Pharoah winning this race took enormous stamina as well as speed. The Belmont was the race where American Pharoah was "crowned."

The win was the fourth attempt at a Triple Crown for trainer Bob Baffert, who at age sixty-two was the second-oldest trainer to win a Triple Crown. It was the third attempt for jockey Victor Espinoza, who was the first Latino jockey to win the Triple Crown, and, at age forty-three, the oldest.

◣ SUGGESTED VIDEOS ◥

A really fun YouTube video to watch is the one of twelve-year-old Chris Taylor describing how he helps on his father's farm, grooming yearlings and caring for them. It's called "A Day in the Life" and was uploaded by Taylor Made Farm on February 22, 2012.

On the Taylor Made Farm website are photos of American Pharoah as a yearling and as a young two-year-old, plus a video of him prior to his standing at auction in Saratoga, New York.

Videos of all his races can be found on the Internet, and you can learn about his early days at Coolmore's Ashford Stud Farm in Kentucky, where he was delivered two days after his Grand Slam win in the Breeders' Cup on October 31, 2015. Coolmore's video "A Horse of a Lifetime" gives a comprehensive, thrilling history of Pharoah's accomplishments.

◣ TRIPLE CROWN WINNERS ◢

1919 SIR BARTON

1930 GALLANT FOX

1935 OMAHA

1937 WAR ADMIRAL

1941 WHIRLAWAY

1943 COUNT FLEET

1946 ASSAULT

1948 CITATION

1973 SECRETARIAT

1977 SEATTLE SLEW

1978 AFFIRMED

2015 AMERICAN PHAROAH

NOTES TO AMERICAN PHAROAH

I am standing yards away from you at the Belmont and can't believe I just watched history being made right before my eyes! I can feel the awe of thousands around me. I know now what it feels like to be a winner, and that has inspired me to be more. To push the distance as you did is motivation for me to push myself. Thank you, American Pharoah.

—MACKENZIE, AGE FIFTEEN

Hello, American Pharoah. You are such an inspiration! What you have done within the first few years of your life is the success many people hope to achieve in their lifetime. And you made it look so easy! You gave me the belief that if I have enough willpower, I can do anything I set my mind to.

Thanks for your stupendous example.

—KALENA, AGE THIRTEEN

I took my little sister to New York to the Belmont on a whim. My sister is one of the most important people in my world. And we got to share precious time together, thanks to you. Being deployed to Afghanistan twice didn't leave me much time to keep in touch with the people I love most. I flew the OH-58D Kiowa Warrior scout helicopter in the army for seven years. It is important to me that my sister truly learns that challenges and hardships have nothing to do with whether or not you can or should do something. Seeing you fly across the finish line at the Belmont was the clearest example of that lesson. You reminded me that doing something most people aren't accustomed to seeing (such as me being a helicopter pilot) is truly worth doing—and can change people's lives. When you won the Belmont, I cried. Everyone cried. Standing there with my sister, watching you win the Triple Crown, which so many never imagined possible again, was awesome! Thank you, Pharoah.

—DEDE, AGE THIRTY-ONE

Thanks for making 2015 a year that I will never forget! Since I have cerebral palsy, my body doesn't work like I would like it to. But I have ridden horses since I was two; and when I was eight, I got interested in the Triple Crown races. I was hooked! Several times I was sure the Triple Crown would be won, but each time I was disappointed with a loss in the Belmont.

So I was so thrilled to watch you win it! And then something even more amazing happened on the morning after you won the Breeders' Cup—I got to meet you! As I approached you, you could tell that something was different about me. But that didn't bother you at all. You lowered your sweet head and let me touch you, and then you made me laugh as you checked my pockets for carrots. You are the grandest horse I will ever meet, but you are also a "regular guy."

I have loved every minute of your journey. Thanks for making 2015 so amazing for me and for so many other people around the world!

—JOSHUA, AGE FIFTEEN

For all of us who, like me, are aiming for a career in animal science, I thank you for what you have taught us. As a high school junior in a vet-assisting magnet program in Alachua County, Florida, I see you as the ultimate example of what breeding, training, and care can produce. We are even more dedicated to bringing the "good life" to all horses.

—SARAH, AGE SEVENTEEN

GLOSSARY

ALPHA HORSE: The leader of a herd, or a horse with the personality that desires to be the leader.

BAY: The color of a horse that is reddish brown with a black mane and tail. The word comes from a Latin word that was the name of a color.

BIT: A stainless-steel, rubber, or aluminum bar attached to the bridle that fits into the horse's mouth, attached to reins. The bit is the means of controlling the horse, following the horseman's old adage "Control the head and the body will follow." The most common racing bit is the D-ring bit, which is shaped like a *D* where it connects to the reins. Different bits address different specific goals, such as preventing bearing in or out as a horse runs.

BLEMISH: A flaw that keeps something from being perfect. The word "blemish" comes from an old French word meaning "to make pale." In the horse world, a blemish means a lump or scar. It may be unsightly, but it does not keep the horse from being sound. The horse is still fit for strenuous work.

BONDING: The love or affection between two animals. The word comes from an old English word meaning "band." Bonding among herd animals gives protection. Bonding between mother and baby provides safety and helps the baby survive. Bonding between horse and trainer or rider means a relationship that works toward a common goal, built on trust.

BREEZING: A horse-racing term meaning to let a horse run at a speed fast enough that the horse has to work really hard. Horsemen in the sport of racing explain breezing as a speed requiring a horse to exert itself. Generally a breeze is ridden under no encouragement, without the use of a whip, just to see if the horse is ready to race and train. An average breeze would be half a mile in forty-eight seconds; three eighths of a mile in thirty-six seconds, a quarter of a mile in twenty-four seconds. Usually the horse is traveling at thirty to forty miles per hour.

CHESTNUT: The color of a horse that is reddish, similar to auburn for a person's hair. Horses also have hard calluses on the inside of their legs, which are referred to as "chestnuts."

CHIFNEY BIT: The gentle bit that is used on yearlings in the auction ring and to accustom them to the use of a regular bit later.

CHROME: The term for white markings on a horse.

CILIA: Hairlike structures that play important parts in an animal's survival, such as eyelashes that protect the eyes. Cilia in the lungs sweep the pathways clean to help the animal breathe in air.

CODA: A passage at the end of a movement or composition in music that brings it to a formal close. From the Italian, meaning "tail," derived from the Latin *cauda*.

COLT: A young male horse that has not been neutered, so he can still have babies. A gelding is a male horse that has been neutered so he cannot have babies. A colt is called a stallion as he gets older and matures. Usually by the age of five, all colts are called stallions. The word "colt" comes from an ancient Swedish word meaning "half-grown animal."

CONFORMATION: The physical makeup, the bodily proportions of a horse—that is, how it is put together.

CORNEA: The thick circular structure covering the lens of the eye that receives light rays to form an image. The horse has three eyelids: upper, lower, and one in the corner that is a membrane, which can be drawn over the eye to protect the cornea. This sort of eyelid can also be seen in a cat.

COVER: A single breeding of a stallion to a mare. Often used as a verb; for example, "He covered fifty mares."

DAM: The mother of an animal, such as a horse. The word "dam" comes from an English word that means "lady."

EOHIPPUS: The extinct animal that is the ancestor of the modern-day horse. It lived more than fifty millions years ago in the Eocene age. It had four toes on each front foot and three toes on each back foot, and was about the size of a fox. The horse eventually got tall over many generations to be able to eat from trees as well as grass from the ground. These changes allowed it to survive.

EQUUS: Meaning "horse," from the Latin word for horse. Also informing the word "equine" used as an adjective. The horse is classified in the phylum Chordata, subphylum Vertebrata, class Mammalia, order Perissodactyla, family Equidae. The family Equidae includes horses, donkeys, and zebras.

FILLY: A young female horse before she has a foal. After a filly is about four years old, she is called a mare.

FLEHMEN: A behavioral response in which a horse opens its mouth and curls up its lip, making it look as though it is smiling. Actually, when a horse does this, it is trying to get a better sense of smell by using the sensitive skin on the inside of its lips. A horse most often uses a flehmen reflex when it smells a strong odor, especially for the first time.

FOAL HEAT: A mare's first estrus period after giving birth. This period of six to eight days is when an egg has been released from a mare's ovary to be fertilized by a stallion. A fertilized egg, known as an embryo, will grow over eleven months into a foal ready to be born. Breeders of racehorses try to catch a mare's foal heat as a prime time for her to become pregnant. She would then have a foal the next year. If a mare does not become pregnant during foal heat, she is said to be "left open," meaning she would not have a foal that year.

FURLONG: A horse-racing term meaning one-eighth of a mile, or 220 yards. The word "furlong" grew from the description of a long furrow, which is the row plowed by a farmer.

INSTINCTS: Behaviors that help animals survive. They are not learned but are present from the moment of birth. Horses are "flight" animals. Without the instinct to run, prey animals would be easy targets for predators, which would kill them for food. Horses are vegetarians; they do not eat meat. Horses are prey for meat-eating animals such as bobcats, tigers, and wolves. Other vegetarian animals, such as deer and cows, do not set off survival alarms within a horse. The word "instinct" comes from an ancient Latin word meaning "to urge on."

LAMINITIS: Inflammation of the sensitive laminae inside the hooves. Laminae is tissue like the skin cells underneath human fingernails. During an attack of laminitis, the laminae begin to tear loose from the rest of the hoof, and the coffin bone (the bottom bone of the foot) may sink down, making it very painful for a horse to bear weight. Laminitis can occur from many causes: stress, overeating, overheating, and chemical changes within the horse's body.

LATHER: Froth formed by profuse sweating.

RATE: When a young Thoroughbred racehorse learns to go different speeds in response to its jockey's signals, it is said to know how to rate.

REGURGITATE: To cause to pour back, to vomit. "Regurgitate" comes from a Latin word, *gurges,* meaning "whirlpool."

SHEDROW: A covered walkway around a barn formed from an overhang of the roof. Shedrow barns are common at racetracks, where the shedrow provides a perfect place to walk a horse for exercise.

SIRE, STUD, STALLION: Terms for male horses. A sire is the father of a foal; he stands "at stud," and a colt becomes a stallion when he matures.

SNAFFLE BIT: The metal bar of the bit is made up of two pieces connected in the middle. The snaffle is free to swivel and is gentle by applying pressure on the outside of a horse's mouth and lips, rather than the roof of the mouth.

STANDING BANDAGES: Wraps on a horse's legs that protect them, sometimes put over a poultice to draw out inflammation, or over liniment to relieve any soreness.

UMBILICAL CORD: The cordlike structure that connects a fetus (unborn foal) with the placenta inside a mare's womb to nourish the foal while it is developing before it is born.

UNGULATE: Having hooves. Hoofed animals such as horses, cattle, deer, swine, and elephants are ungulate mammals.

VESTIGIAL: A trace of an organ or part in an organism that is a remnant of a former developmental stage. Splint bones in a modern horse are a vestigial part of the toes in the prehistoric horse, the eohippus.

WEANLING: A foal that is no longer nursing milk from its mother.

SOURCES

Associated Press. "American Pharoah Wins Preakness, Sets Up Triple Crown Shot." *New York Post*, May 16, 2015.

Bekoff, Mark. *The Emotional Lives of Animals*. Novato, CA: New World Library, 2007.

Bennett, James. "Centerville's Jill Baffert: 'It's a Wonderful Life' with Bob Baffert, American Pharoah, Triple Crown." *Columbia* (Tennessee) *Daily Herald*, June 28, 2015.

"Bob Baffert." biography.com.

Brown, Alex. Posts by the exercise rider and writer. alexbrownracing.com.

Carson, Dan. "Bob Baffert's 10-Year-Old Son Went Absolutely Nuts Watching American Pharoah Win." bleacherreport.com, May 2, 2015.

Crawford, Eric. "Preakness: From Humble Beginnings to Riding Chrome." *Pittsburgh Post-Gazette*, May 17, 2014.

Culpepper, Chuck. "For Victor Espinoza, the Man in 'Pharoah's' Saddle, Riding Roots Run Deep." *Washington Post*, June 4, 2015.

Day, Steve. "Before American Pharoah Became a National Name, He Earned His Stripes at a Training Center in Ocala." *The Village Daily Sun*, July 26, 2015.

DePaolo, Joe. "Pony Smokey a Loyal American Pharoah Sidekick." *The Blood-Horse*, June 4, 2015.

Drape, Joe. "Ahmed Zayat's Journey." *New York Times*, June 4, 2015.

Drape, Joe. *American Pharoah*. New York: Hachette Books, 2016.

Drape, Joe. "Kentucky Derby 2015: American Pharoah Wins a Close Race." *New York Times*, May 2, 2015.

Forde, Pat. "American Pharoah Owner Ahmed Zayat Is Living the Dream, but Still Looking for Derby Glory." Sports.yahoo.com, May 1, 2015.

Fox Sports, Facebook post on the Breeders' Cup, October 31, 2015.

Gruen, Seth. "After American Pharoah, Victor Espinoza Can't Outrun Fame." *Rolling Stone*, June 11, 2015.

Harris, Beth. "Owner Ahmed Zayat Takes Aim at Kentucky Derby with 3 Horses." Associated Press, April 27, 2015.

Harris, Susan E. *The United States Pony Club Manual of Horsemanship, C Level*. New York: Wiley Publishing, Inc., 1995.

"Horse Racing." EncyclopediaBritannica.com.

Hurcomb, Michael. "American Pharoah Has First Workout Friday Since Preakness Win." cbssports.com, May 22, 2015.

"Kentucky Derby Point System." AllHorseRacing.ag.

Layden, Tim. "All American Pharoah." *Sports Illustrated*, June 15, 2015.

Louisville Courier-Journal articles posted by Jonathan Lintner, Tim Sullivan, and Jennie Rees, May–August, 2015.

McCarthy, Cormac. *All the Pretty Horses*. New York: Vintage Books, 1993, p. 6.

McKathan Brothers Farm Facebook page, in particular the YouTube video taken at McKathan Brothers Farm, March, 2014. Posted by Cynthia Mikell, featuring breeze rider Susan Montanye.

McNamara, Ed. "Bob Baffert's Heart Attack Put Winning Races in Perspective." *Newsday*, May 12, 2015.

O'Hara, Mary. *My Friend Flicka*. New York: HarperCollins, 2003. First published in 1941. pp. 129–130.

Petrella, Steve. "How Did American Pharoah Get His Misspelled Name"? Sporting news.com, April 29, 2015.

Phelan, Kevin. "Q&A with Triple Crown–Winning Jockey Victor Espinoza." *Journal News*, July 28, 2015.

Privman, Jay. "Bob Baffert Recovering from Heart Attack in Dubai." *Daily Racing Form*, March 28, 2012.

Reagan, Ronald. *An American Life*. New York: Simon & Schuster, 1990.

Rees, Jennie. "American Pharoah Wins Kentucky Derby 2015." *Courier-Journal* (Louisville, KY), May 3, 2015.

Rees, Jennie. "Five Reasons Why American Pharoah Will and Won't Win Triple Crown." *USA Today*, May 4, 2015.

Roberts, Monty. *The Man Who Listens to Horses*. New York: Random House, 1996, especially pp. 231–236.

Rogers, Byron. "The Stride of a Champion: How Does American Pharoah Compare to Secretariat?" performancegenetics.com, June 12, 2015.

Rosenblatt, Richard. "Lessons Learned from American Pharoah's Preakness Victory." Associated Press, May 17, 2015.

"Special Report: American Pharoah, Making History." *Equus*, November 2015, pp. 26–36.

Sullivan, Tim. "Espinoza a Hard Sell Despite Derby Success." *Courier-Journal* (Louisville, KY), May 16, 2014.

The New Columbia Encyclopedia. New York: Columbia University Press, 1975, pp. 1272–1273.

Tompkins, Courtney. "Triple Crown–Winning Jockey Victor Espinoza on His Life-Changing Ride." *Pasadena Star-News*, June 15, 2015.

Victor Espinoza on *Charlie Rose*, TV show, YouTube.com.

Wharton, David. "Bob Baffert Has Come a Long Way in Horse Racing." *Los Angeles Times*, June 5, 2015.

Wilson, Art. "A Little Luck Goes a Long Way for Jockey Victor Espinoza." *Los Angeles Daily News*, June 18, 2015.

ABOUT THE AUTHOR

SHELLEY FRASER MICKLE has published more than a dozen books that, along with her commitment to literacy and the power of story, led to her being nominated to the Florida Women's Hall of Fame in 2014. Her publications have been *New York Times* Notable Books and *Library Journal*'s Best Adult Books. Her nonfiction book, *Barbaro: America's Horse*, won a Bank Street Award. She lives on her ranch in Gainesville, Florida.